To You,

Contents

Introduction

At some point in our lives, each one of us has wandered around some small countryside road, hopelessly lost. And when finding a local farmer from whom to ask directions, been told: "Oh! If I were you and wanting to go to X, I wouldn't start from here!"

Investing can often feel that way. Which is why having some kind of road-map is helpful. The following book is an attempt to provide just such a roadmap in the hope that, even if our reader remains unsure of where he is heading, at least he will know where he stands.

The following chapters represent "our roadmap", and by ours, I mean GaveKal's. Indeed, although I am putting this book together, most of the ideas in the following pages have come from our clients, or were developed by my business partners Charles and Pierre Gave, Anatole Kaletsky, Steven Vannelli, Alfred Ho, Ahmad Abdallah and Arthur Kroeber - over the course of conversations, research reports and seminar presentations. Very few of the ideas actually come from me. I am thus deeply indebted to all my GaveKal colleagues and clients.

When we started GaveKal in 1998, the three initial partners (Charles, Anatole and myself) agreed on little (especially politics) but one thing: the fact that we were living in revolutionary times. For some reason, it seems that the years at the turn of the century are prone to important changes. Consider the following:

- A man who fell asleep in 1790 and woke up in 1820 would have found the World a very different place: the ideals of the American

Revolution were spreading, the French Revolution had come and gone, Napoleon had slaughtered a whole generation of young European males, factories and mines were springing up, industry was replacing agriculture as the motor of the economy in Britain....

- A man who fell asleep in 1890 would have found a very different world in 1920: the Ottoman, Hapsburg, Romanov and Qing dynasties had all come crashing down. The United States was now the main power in the Western World, and Japan was the main power in the East. Germany was on its knees and France and Italy were not doing much better....

- A man who fell asleep in 1990 will already find a very different world than the one he left behind: no more Soviet Union or communist threat but a simmering clash of civilizations, a once economically all-powerful Japan reduced to the rank of also-rans, a China struggling with internal contradictions but still emerging as the World's second largest economic power, information transmitted from one end of the globe to another at the press of a button, the human genome mapped....

Reviewing our recent History further convinces me that something deeply structural is happening in our markets. To illustrate this, I will make an honest confession: if someone had come up to me eight years ago and told me that we would experience:

- A 75% wipeout on the Nasdaq,

- 9/11 and the anthrax attacks,

- Wars in Afghanistan and Iraq,

- Enron,

- Follow-up terrorist attacks in Madrid, Istanbul, London, Mumbai...,

- SARS & bird flu,

- Oil at US$110/bl,

- GM debt downgraded to junk (remember that GM is the fourth largest corporate bond issuer in the World after the US, Japanese and Italian governments),

- Katrina,

- Refco (the biggest commodity broker) imploding in the space of a week,

- A big conflict between Israel and Hezbollah that Israel would not win,

- The first year-on-year fall in US house prices in fifty years,

- The biggest loss in hedge fund History (Amaranth), and biggest trading fraud (SG) on record.

- A nuclear bomb detonation in North Korea…,

- Write-offs of hundreds of billions of dollars across our financial industries…,

- Bear stearns, Northern Rock, Countrywide, IKB…

I would have likely concluded that the best thing to do was to head to my lake house in Oklahoma, load up on guns, cartridges, canned goods and bottled water and wait it out… If that same person had told me that, in the US and in most other countries, corporate profits would be reaching record highs and that a number of markets, including the Dow Jones, the Hang Seng, the Indian Sensex, Brazil, Australia, Indonesia…would, in that same period, be hitting all-time highs, while the VIX index was hitting all-time lows, I would definitely have called for the men in white coats with the van and the padded room.

But was it all a willing temporary suspension of disbelief on the part of investors? Are the chickens finally coming home to roost? The fact that January 2008 was the worst January ever recorded for almost all global equity markets and the fact that real estate markets in most OECD countries seem to now be heading south may point in that direction. The general media is definitely full of enough doom and gloom to help one think that the world is coming to an end.

The recent lack of stability across financial markets led legendary investor George Soros to proclaim that we are now facing "the worst market crisis in 60 years" *(Financial Times, January 23rd 2008)*. In his article, George Soros offers the clearest and most persuasive "case for the prosecution" explaining how the world economy and financial system got into the present crisis.

Soros' first insight is that this crisis is more than just a typical boom-bust cycle, of the kind often experienced by financial markets. This cycle, he contends, marks the climax of a 60-year boom in consumer borrowing and credit growth. This has produced excesses in banking, asset values and financial innovation which will take years, or even decades, to unwind. Economies addicted to easy credit will be devastated as their banking systems now suffer a long-term decline, which is what Soros' 60-year "super-cycle" inevitably implies.

Soros' second insight is that the reversal of "the 60-year super-boom" in credit will damage America more than other economies and will thus end the global dominance of the dollar and shift the balance of power in the world economy to the creditor countries of Asia and the Middle East. Both these points are absolutely valid, but **the reversal of credit growth, the slowdown in US consumption and the shift in economic power towards Asia are a matter of degree. They will all undoubtedly happen, but there is no reason to suppose—and no evidence so far— that these shifts will be so abrupt as to cause a serious recession**, still less the greatest economic crisis of the past 60 years.

Soros' third, and most important, insight is that the two economic super-cycles he describes–in global credit and in US consumption–were themselves part of an even bigger super-cycle in politics and ideology. The excesses of financial innovation and consumer spending were encouraged by financial deregulation, based on an ideological belief that the market was always right and could solve its own problems. This ideology of "market fundamentalism" ignored, in Soros' view, the fundamental driving force of all boom-bust cycles, a process he calls "reflexivity". Because markets are driven not by reality but by investors' often misguided views about reality, prices tend to overshoot on the way up (when everyone is too bullish) and also on the way down. But as investors chase prices up (and then down), they change economic reality and thereby justify their own expectations. This is the process now threatening the world economy: the collapse of confidence in the US banking system is changing reality and causing a recession which, in turn, will justify investors' fears of further catastrophic deterioration in the banks.

This is one roadmap. Ours is different.

In *The End is Not Nigh*, a book published in late 2006, we concluded with the following thoughts: *"Ever since the start of the late 20th Century's great global expansion, many politicians, economists, and media commentators have been issuing dire warnings about the economic retribution which surely lies ahead after so many years of overindulgence in consumption, speculation and borrowing.*

But there are many reasons for doubting such prophecies of doom… The first is that the Prophets of Doom have predicted their day of reckoning, like Jehovah's Witnesses, at the beginning of almost every year since the mid-1980s. And every time their predictions have turned out to be wrong, they have merely redoubled their warnings about the terrifying instability of the world economy. Instead of accepting that this argument had been refuted, they have insisted that financial or political manipulations have simply held off the collapse, thereby guaranteeing an even more wrathful Dies Irae when the reckoning finally arrives.

In arguing that postponing economic problems automatically magnifies these dangers, the Jehovah's Witness economists have misunderstood the most important virtue of a liberal, competitive economy—the fact that it automatically encourages billions of intelligent, motivated and creative individuals to seek out solutions to whatever economic challenges the world may present. **In a competitive global economy, therefore, time is on the side of stability, not against it.** *If governments refrain from tackling potential problems, in the way in which America, for example, has refrained from tackling the "unsustainable" trade deficits or Britain has refrained from tackling the "dangerous" level of mortgage borrowing, this does not automatically increase the potential danger.* **In a liberal, competitive world, a problem postponed is not necessarily magnified.** *On the contrary, a problem postponed is a problem well on the way to being solved.*

Another, less philosophical, reason to ignore the Prophets of Doom has been their failure to understand the underlying forces which have powered the expansion of the global economy since the early 1990s. Specifically, there have been four:

- *Firstly, the collapse of communism, which has given three billion new consumers and producers the opportunity to enjoy the economic benefits of capitalism.*

- *Secondly, the spread of free trade, which has allowed these new capitalists to participate in the global economy for the first time.*

- *Thirdly, advances in electronic technology, which have cut communication costs almost to zero.*

- *Fourthly, a revolution in finance which has given consumers the freedom to manage both their assets and their borrowings, in a way that was once only possible for large multinational companies.*

While some of these structural changes may seem to increase the risks in financial markets, their interaction has actually made the global economy more stable than ever before. For example, the shift of manufacturing employment from America to China has created huge trade imbalances. But the same globalisation process has made global trade imbalances easier to finance, and the shift from manufacturing to services in the US and in other advanced economies has made them more stable than ever before. This greater stability, in turn, has reduced the risks of household borrowing; and the freedom of households to borrow has made consumption more stable in the face of economic shocks, such as the collapse of technology shares or the terrorist attacks of 9/11.

*Economists (ourselves included) are still far from understanding the full implications of all these changes—or of weighing them up against new long-term dangers such as climate change, demographic decline and widening disparities of income. We can, however, say one thing for certain: this year, the Jehovah's Witness economists will yet again be proven wrong. **The End is Not Nigh.** "*

Since we penned these words, a lot has happened. For a start, and as highlighted by George Soros in his article, the credit cycle is no longer in an ascendance phase. Needless to say, this is a very important change. But is it a cyclical event? Or a structural turning point?

We have argued at length over recent years that one of the driving forces of financial markets was the "financial revolution" which was quietly moving from the US and other Anglo-Saxon countries unto the rest of the world. Today, this financial revolution seems to be, at the very least, "put on hold". So what impact should that have on our investment decisions?

Moreover, this is not the only important change to occur to our roadmap since we published *Our Brave New World (2005)* and *The End is Not Nigh (2006)*. As we write, we are seeing some important policy changes in the US, Europe, but especially in Asia. These should be incorporated into any thinking about financial markets.

Given all of the above, I thought it made sense, as much for myself as for our research clients, to lay out my current investment roadmap. And I do this in three very simple, and separate parts. The first part of the book reviews what I believe are the "four revolutionary megatrends" currently reshaping our global economy. The second part focuses on what I believe are the very important policy changes and their impact on the financial markets. The third part highlights what I think all this means for investments over the coming quarters.

Before digging into the coming chapters, I would like to highlight two important disclaimers and two words of caution:

The first disclaimer is that the book aggregates some of the ideas that have been published over the years in our research. So a lot of the passages will go through have actually been written by my colleagues Charles Gave, Anatole Kaletsky, Arthur Kroeber and Steven Vannelli. Thus, I am less the author of this book than its chief "cut and paster"!

The second disclaimer is that the section on emerging markets is really a section about China and its impact on the global economy. In my head, I justify this by arguing that "China is by far the most important of emerging markets". But the reality, of course, is that while I feel very confident talking about China (especially thanks to all the tremendous information and original thoughts that Arthur Kroeber passes on to me regularly), I do not know nearly enough on Russia, Brazil, India, Africa, Turkey, Saudi Arabia… to speak about those important countries intelligently. Having mentioned Arthur Kroeber, I should again point out that a lot of the work on China in this book comes directly from him and his team at GaveKal-Dragonomics in Beijing.

The first word of caution is that, since some of the passages in this book have previously appeared as GaveKal or Dragonomics research reports, some of the material presented over the coming pages will be very familiar to our most faithful readers. For this I apologize.

The second word of caution is that, in some of the chapters below, I will tend to use 'we' to describe beliefs and ideas. When I do use "we", the reader should see this as meaning GaveKal and not assume that I am the most pompous author they have ever come across. In other chapters, I will use "I"; this may be because I am relating personal experiences, or ideas, that my colleagues do not share. I fully realize that this switching between "I" and "we" will likely get tedious. For this I apologize. I guess, unlike Schumpeter, I do not aim to also be the world's best writer *(Schumpeter would often say: "I aim to be the world's best economist, best writer, best horseman and best lover". After a pause, he would then add "I am not doing so well with the horses").*

Structural Megatrends

The Importance of the Financial Revolution–the Theory

One of the longest running themes in our research (a theme which pre-dates our fascination with China's growth or the emergence of "platform-companies" - see *Our Brave New World*) was that the changes in the "money world" were having a massive impact on both our economies and our financial markets. Basically, since the early 1990s, the Western world has experienced nothing short of a massive financial revolution with the birth of dozens of new financial instruments: REITS, derivatives, futures contracts, options, credit-default swaps, re-mortgages, junk bonds… And all these instruments, were partly at the source of the past twenty year's boom.

As we look at it, junk bonds and Michael Milken were really the match that got everything started. Before Milken came around, companies around the world typically had two avenues to obtain capital: tap the equity markets or turn to commercial bankers and ask for a loan. When, in the mid-1980's, Milken invented the junk bond market, he all of a sudden gave companies the ability to bypass banks when financing their growth and diversify (and thus stabilize) their sources of funding.

Shortly thereafter, we started to witness a proliferation in derivatives products that allowed companies to hedge certain risks (i.e.: exchange rates, commodity prices, interests rates…) at a very minimal cost. In turn, this allowed for a lower volatility of earnings. As the use of these new financial instruments began spreading (initially just in the US, then around the Anglo-Saxon World, and then everywhere), we started to witness some interesting developments.

For a start, the volatility of growth in the Western world started to fall and the economic cycle became much smoother. In recent years, this has been dubbed "the great moderation" and all sorts of papers have been published on the importance of this collapse in the volatility of growth. And sure enough, an environment where the economic cycle is tamer is highly beneficial to companies, and to their employees. Indeed, the lack of volatility in the cycle helps companies manage more efficiently and invest effectively for a more stable outcome. In contrast, a volatile economic cycle provokes bankruptcies across the board as numerous industries are incapable of keeping up with orders in the good times and incapable of finding business in the bad times. In turn, this creates layoffs, redundancies, etc....

Because wild swings in the economic cycle provoke bankruptcies, the demise of the banking multiplier has been welcome news for equity markets, especially the weakest players (i.e.: small caps). With the threat of bankruptcies linked to the economic cycle receding, the "equity premium" which investors needed to hold cycle-sensitive assets or small-caps shrank, and we experienced roaring bull markets across global equity markets.

But it is not just in the financing of company projects that the revolution has had a big impact. The financial revolution has also allowed companies to protect their assets, and their future profits, against potential threats- and this regardless of the size of the company. Indeed, a few years ago, only the biggest multinationals could beat up commercial banks into doing what they needed. Today, anyone has the ability to hedge his exchange rate risk, his commodity risk, his interest rate risk... or whatever risk associated with the business. This ability to hedge future risks might help explain why, in recent cycles, corporate profit volatility has fallen and the overall level of profits has increased. The blossoming of the financial revolution might also help explain why, in recent years, almost everywhere around the world, small caps have outperformed large caps massively. Indeed it used to be that large caps had a serious advantage over small caps: financial clout. The CFO of a large company could call any bank and say: "I would like you to do this, that, and the other for me", to which the commercial banker would typically reply "but, yes, of course". Meanwhile, the CFO of a small company would be told: "excuse me Sir while I put you on hold". Now, thanks to the financial revolution, even the smallest of tiny companies can call any commercial bank and get a competitive price for whatever it needs done. The financial playing field has evened out.

The financial revolution started in the mid 1980s in the US, and then rapidly spread to the Anglo Saxon countries. And as the financial revolution spread its wings, these countries (the US, UK, Australia and Canada) were typically described as "living beyond their means" and set for a "day of reckoning"… But interestingly, since 1991, three of these four countries have not experienced a recession (though, prior to that, they use to experience a recession every four to six years). The country that did experience a recession, the US in 2001, ended up living through the shallowest recession in its modern history (more importantly, the recession would most likely have been avoided had it not been for the terrorist attacks of 9/11). Of course, we might be drawing a causal link where there is none. **Nevertheless, the fact remains that recessions now seem to be more infrequent, and shallower, than they did in the past.**

A fall in the volatility of growth, and in the volatility of a company's earnings, is great news for the consumer, if for no other reason that he gets to keep his job instead of losing it at the bottom of the cycle. Indeed, when the cycle is very violent, all too often, labor is the variable of adjustment; at the bottom of the economic cycle, when companies' profits have melted away and the banks are calling in loans, companies have little choice but to let go of employees. Today, thanks to a better optimization of balance sheets, and a risk-management approach to earnings, the tough redundancy decisions that most managers do not like to take need not be taken as frequently as in the past. And this is not the only way the consumer has benefited from the financial revolution.

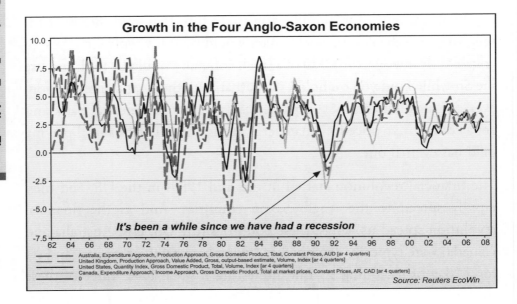

Growth in the Four Anglo-Saxon Economies

It's been a while since we have had a recession

Australia, Expenditure Approach, Production Approach, Gross Domestic Product, Total, Constant Prices, AUD [ar 4 quarters]
United Kingdom, Production Approach, Value Added, Gross, output-based estimate, Volume, Index [ar 4 quarters]
United States, Quantity Index, Gross Domestic Product, Total, Volume, Index [ar 4 quarters]
Canada, Expenditure Approach, Income Approach, Gross Domestic Product, Total at market prices, Constant Prices, AR, CAD [ar 4 quarters]
0

Source: Reuters EcoWin

The exciting thing in recent years has been that the emergence of continuously more efficient information systems has allowed the benefits of the financial revolution to accrue to the large companies as well as smaller companies and the man in the street. Today, any individual in the US (or Australia, Spain, the Netherlands, Sweden, the UK…) with some assets can use them to borrow from a bank, and choose from a menu the liability that he will put in front of this asset. **An individual can optimize his balance sheet in a way that would have been impossible for a multinational firm one generation ago!** Now this has had a massive immediate financial impact. If assets which for years had laid dormant and illiquid (i.e.: a house in Paris, an apartment in Hong Kong…) are all of a sudden, thanks to new financial tools, transformed into liquid assets, then two things occur:

- A lot of money that had previously been tied down is released to flow into consumption, activity, financial markets…

- The attributes of real estate as an asset class change. Instead of being a boring, highly illiquid investment, real estate becomes an asset from which it is possible to draw liquidity quite easily. This makes real estate far less unattractive than it used to be and the illiquidity/risk premium attached to real estate drops... We then witness a re-rating of real estate assets. This is what has happened in every country where the financial revolution has taken hold, whether the US, Australia, the UK, Spain or the Netherlands...

Of course, this was the theory. In practice, as we know today, massive excesses took place, at least in the US but probably in Spain, Ireland, Denmark, Holland, the UK, Australia... as well. Individuals and companies with no balance sheets, or income, were allowed to leverage to levels defying any common sense. Meanwhile, banks told us that the loans provided did not reside on their balance sheets. Instead, the loans were packaged into structured products, and sold on to yield-seeking entities (pension funds, endowments, insurance companies, hedge funds...) whose time-horizon, and risk appetites, matched that of the product. Of course, we now know that this was hogwash and that the structured products had indeed left the banks' balance sheets, but only to go sit in off-balance sheet vehicles while everyone thought that such vehicles had gone out of fashion after Enron. Of course, as trouble started and the people who should not have been lent money to buy overvalued homes began defaulting on their loans, the "off-balance sheet" liabilities came back very rapidly onto the books, and the banks had to take massive write-offs.

This is where we are today. So do the excesses of recent years, and their current unwinding, mean that the financial revolution is over?

Putting the Current Credit Crunch in Context

I live in Asia. Consequently, I frequently find myself stopped in the middle of the street by a local "entrepreneur" who offers me a Hermes tie for US$5, or a Longines watch for US$10. I always walk away because, deep down, I suspect that there is something wrong, and that the product on offer might not be the genuine article. I also imagine that I am not alone in making this assumption.

When I am not walking down the street, I am usually studying financial markets. And there, to my surprise, a lot of fake Hermes ties and Longines watches have been sold as genuine articles to customers that were either stupid, accomplices, or both, in what might have been one of the greatest swindles of all time.

Let me explain: if instead of selling ties, my local entrepreneur had been trying to sell me a corporate bond, he would have approached me and said: "Look here in my bag. Underneath the cabbage, I have a beautiful AAA bond, which yields 6.5% instead of 4.5%…" I would hope that my alarm bells would have gone off, and that I would have suspected that something fishy was going on. In other words, as for the Hermes ties and the Longines watches, I would have assumed that these bonds were not the genuine article.

As a rule, when someone tries to sell me something with a totally abnormal profitability, given the apparent risk, I become immediately suspicious. My suspicion turns into genuine panic if, on top of it, the seller is willing to "guarantee" either a return significantly above the government bond yield, or a return of my capital regardless of what has happened in the markets, at any time. So I knew that there was something wrong in the subprime market, but I had better things to do than to try to understand these very complex products (namely, make money the old-fashioned way by buying equities and holding onto them as if my life depended on it).

In his book *Quantum Investing*, my friend Steve Waite explains that there are two kinds of risks in the markets: "Exogenous Risk," which is risk that comes from outside events, and "Endogenous Risk," which is risk that has built up internally. The terrible events of 9/11 were exogenous, as was SARS in Hong Kong. The crash of 1987 was endogenous; as was the TMT bust of 2000.

Most investors spend a lot of time worrying about exogenous risks. At GaveKal, I frequently field questions on the threat of Iran, or North Korea, or bird-flu, or climate change... all issues on which very frankly, I have little wisdom to share. Meanwhile, most big bear markets tend to be the result of endogenous risk. No one yells fire in the movie theater. It just gets too crowded. The tipping point tips. Someone moves toward the door, and suddenly it's too late. As my much-missed friend Hunt Taylor put it to me once: "The final dynamic is the almost unanimous opinion that exists prior to the event. Even when most of us know better, we tend not to act. Stocks in '87 and '99, the carry trade in '94 - we knew these markets weren't going to go on forever, but, lemminglike, we marched steadfastly cliffward!"

Having had the opportunity of working in the financial markets for some years, I would have to concur with my friend Hunt. Most of the bear markets I have witnessed (Japan, Asia, TMT, US real estate...) have been more of an "endogenous" than "exogenous" nature. But I would go a step further than Steve Waite and argue that, within endogenous bear markets, one typically finds two categories:

- The bear markets created by governments, usually because one, or several, of what we have called in our research *The Five Cardinal*

Sins (protectionism, tax increases, monetary policy mistakes, regulatory overkill or war) are committed. Japan in the 1990s comes to mind...

- The bear markets triggered by the market participants themselves, usually because of the belief in some kind of a "Ponzi scheme" (Ponzi was that ingenious investor who was guaranteeing a very high return and paid the returns to the old members by borrowing from the new members. As long as the entries are higher than the exits, the system grows; but then, of course, it collapses when it moves into negative cash flows...).

The current subprime debacle falls mostly into the second category of bear markets, though it was also partly a result of silly regulations imposed on pension funds, insurance companies and the like. In that respect, it resembles the turn off the century bull-bear market, which was in large part triggered by the push towards indexation.

A good Ponzi scheme always start with an "abnormally" high rate of return, "guaranteed" by a fairly respectable institution or individual. It also fulfills a need. With that framework in mind, let me review the current subprime debacle.

From 2000 to 2003, we had a huge bear market in equities, created by the previous Ponzi scheme called indexation (see *Our Brave New World*, which the reader can download for free at www.gavekal.com). As a result of the indexation craze and the following bear market, pension funds and insurance companies around the world found themselves undercapitalized. The regulators, always keen to close the barn door once the horses have fled, decided to prevent the undercapitalized institutions from buying any more equities. This left pension funds and insurance companies with a pressing need: how to replace equities, the high return part of their portfolios? Since, according to the new regulations, they could only buy bonds, they were forced, if they wanted to boost returns, to buy very low quality bonds, offering very high immediate returns (yields).

The problem was of course that the regulators had told them that they could not buy bonds below "investment grade" (whatever that was)… and that, as a result of the massive demand for yield around the world, the returns on investment grade bonds were far below the returns on equities that they now had to replace…. So all of a sudden, here was a new need: **the low quality bond with a high rating.**

Now the beauty of capitalism is that a demand usually does not have to wait too long until a supply emerges. And if this is true on Main Street, it is true in spades on Wall Street. **If I have learned just one thing in my career, it is that Wall Street will always find a way to satisfy a demand!** The supply of financial products will always rise to meet the demand, as the elasticity of production on Wall-Street is, I believe, infinite….

In the late 1990s (the indexation bull-bear market), the work-load fell on consultants and indexers. This time around, it fell on the rating agencies, and the houses specialized in the financing of homes (derivative products). As a result of this new demand, the wizards on Wall Street started to work feverishly.

My father always tells me: "I have never met a simulation that did not look great." And sure enough, the mathematical geniuses in charge of building new products started to "design" portfolios of mortgages, mixing them in a way that, in the past, would have guaranteed the high returns needed, and the repayment of the principal at the end.

The fact that the historical sample on which they built their computations had nothing to do with the current issues was of course never discussed. The ratings agencies, impressed by the soundness of the computation, and even more by the huge fees that they were getting for rating these (toxic) products, started to deliver "investment grade" ratings to products that had never met a (free) market, not paying enough attention perhaps to the slight conflict of interest that they could have. And before you knew it, the problem was solved: we had, at last, a junk bond with a AAA rating!

Once again, it seems that everything started with a regulatory or political intervention, forcing a change in the asset or liability side of the balance sheets of financial institutions, without changing the other side. Preventing insurance companies or pension funds from buying equities at the bottom of a bear market was a mistake of massive proportions. This decision reduced future returns, without reducing future costs (since they are a function of contracts, signed long before the intervention).

The reality of the capitalistic system is, however, fairly easy for all to see. Basically, the system offers returns spread around three anchors (for a diversified portfolio):

- 1% real: For those who cannot afford any kind of volatility, they have to buy 3 month T-bills, in their own currency.

- 3% real: For those willing to take a duration risk, but no risk on the return *of* capital, they have to buy long-dated government bonds.

- 6% real: For those willing to forfeit the reimbursement of their capital (no guaranteed return *of* capital or *on* capital), and are willing to take the equity risk. They, over time and in the absence of massive policy mistakes, earn a much higher return on capital.

Let us imagine an insurance company which signed contracts based on expectations of 4.5% real returns. It will, logically, have invested 50% in equities and 50% in long-dated bonds. Now let us imagine that, suddenly the regulator comes in and tells our insurance company not to own any, or at least much less, equities. Our insurance company will thus have to either:

a) move up considerably on the risk scale in the bond market, thereby replacing the volatility risk of equities with the default risk of junk bonds - a terrible trade-off in my humble opinion, or

b) move up the duration scale considerably and cross its fingers that its duration bet (at a time of very low rates) pays off.

Of course, we now know that both options unfolded. As mentioned above, the financial system moved in fairly quickly to satisfy the new demand. And sure enough, returns were abnormally high in this new and very profitable activity.

Unfortunately, however, at some point reality always sets in and Ponzi goes to jail. Forced selling then takes over. And this, of course, is what has been happening in recent months.

Indeed, insurance companies, banks and other financial institutions are loaded with different kinds of financial instruments. On OECD government bonds, there are no reserve requirements. On corporate bonds, the requirements vary with the rankings. AAA bonds have very low reserve requirements, junk bonds much higher. In some countries, reserve requirements on equities are 100%, and the portfolios must be marked to markets at the end of every year (or quarter).

Given that insurance companies and banks bought a lot of the synthetic bonds ranked AAA by the agencies, as the agencies start downgrading the paper, the financial companies have to sell these bonds–except that they are not sellable! They are then forced to aggressively sell their equities, buy government bonds and keep the cash, regardless of the prices reached by the equities or the bonds. They need to do this solely to satisfy their legal requirements.

For this reason, one of the golden rules of bear markets is that typically, people sell not what they should (in today's case, sub-prime bonds) but what they can (today, equities). It is for this reason that old market hands always say that the only thing that goes up in a credit crunch is correlation.

I thus sincerely believe that the recent collapse in global equity markets has a lot less to do with the economy or the earnings of the companies, and everything to do with the fact that financial companies everywhere are breaching their reserve requirements and have no choice but to present the market with massive sell orders on equities and buy orders on bonds.

This, of course, leaves us with a question: how many Ponzi schemes will we need to live through before regulators and politicians stop intervening in financial markets and institutions to "improve" the situation? On this one, I fear that the news is not encouraging. Few politicians in the US or Europe today seem to share the wisdom of Lord Salisbury who, when prompted by Queen Victoria to institute various changes, replied: "Change, Your Majesty? Don't you think that things are bad enough as they are?" Unfortunately, it seems that, today, there are few Lord Salisbury's in the halls of power. Instead, most view the current credit crunch as a reason to expand regulation, and government control, over the economy.

Our fear is thus not that the credit crunch means the end of the financial revolution. But instead that the credit crunch will invite an increase in regulation, which in turn will mean the end of the financial revolution.

The Financial Revolution Hits a Road-Bump–But Will It Bounce Back?

Following the sustained downturn of US housing and the debacle on sub-prime loans and asset-backed commercial paper, questions are of course being raised as to the sustainability of the securitization movement. So have recent developments put the financial revolution at risk? Our belief is: not a bit. And this for the following reasons:

1. Nobody ever questions the long-term sustainability of the stock market because, once in a while, we have a bear market in equities. Why should it be different for the credit markets?

2. The populations of almost all rich nations are aging and will thus increasingly need long-dated assets with a regular stream of income. Simultaneously, with most Western companies in positive cash flow (as heavy-duty capital spending gets moved to emerging markets–more on that later) and with more and more governments in budget surpluses, there are reasons to think that the usual debt-issuers will not be sufficient to meet a growing need for fixed income. The pension needs of the future will have to be covered by new issuers.

3. Which takes us to our third point: the issuers of mortgages do not need to be in the same country as the buyers. Indeed, today, a mortgage can be issued in Brazil, hedged into the Swedish Krona, and bought by a Swedish pension fund. This allows Swedish retirees to get their income from the much younger population of Brazil.

27

We believe that the financial revolution is still in its infancy, and that the future for new structured financial products remains very bright. In fact, the events of the past two months remind us of the beginning of program trading in the equity markets in the middle of the 1980s. Program trading led to the strange idea of "portfolio insurance", which subsequently triggered the crash of 1987. At that time, anyone who stopped investing on the idea that program trading was doomed (because of the crash), would have missed the indexation movement, the creation of ETFs, the "quant" way of managing money (which, during these past six months, some of our readers probably wish they had missed), the growth of arbitrage funds, hedge funds, etc...

The same argument can be made for the credit markets today. We are only at the beginning of a bewildering increase in the use and tradability of credit products. We are undeniably facing a bear market in credit. And bear markets can last for several quarters or even years (this one most likely will); but just like 1987 did not mark the end for equities, August 2007 will not mark the end of the financial revolution. In fact, political meddling and grand-standing aside, the current crisis should allow the system to redevelop itself more soundly, around more market-based pricing rather than the flawed model-based pricing of the past.

Going a step further, we have been through credit crunches and serious banking crises before. In 1990-91, the US Savings & Loans industry went belly-up. At the same time, the Japanese bear market started. In 1991-92, numerous Scandinavian financial institutions teetered on the verge of bankruptcy. In 1994, France's Debit Lyonnais hit the wall. In 1997, banks in Korea, Indonesia, Thailand flirted with insolvency. In 2000, Turkey faced a serious financial squeeze...

Looking back at these events, it seems obvious to us that there is a simple way to deal with a credit crunch (there is also a Japanese way–though that one is not recommended). In essence, once its banking system seizes up, a country should follow the following three-step plan:

Step #1: Devalue the currency massively. This makes your domestic risk assets (real estate, equities…) attractive to foreigners and encourages capital inflows. It also makes your goods more attractive and rapidly leads to an increase in the trade balance. The combination of capital inflows and improving trade balance means that the "cash crunch" can then abate.

Step #2: Re-capitalize the banks. As Japan has nicely demonstrated over the past fifteen years, it is very hard to have a well-functioning economy without a well-capitalized banking system. Now if banks have handed out a bunch of stupid loans then recapitalizing the banks may mean wiping out the existing shareholders. So be it. This is what Sweden did in 1992 and France did in 1994 with Credit Lyonnais. It is also what the UK will most likely end up having to do with Northern Rock. But one thing is important here: the recapitalization should happen quickly. The longer one waits, the more the rot can spread.

Step #3: Put in a steep yield curve. Once recapitalized, it is not a guarantee that the banks will go out and lend. In fact, they will most likely be too shell-shocked by the recent credit crunch to do anything but sit on their hands. Because of this, having a steep yield curve is important: it encourages the banks to go out and multiply their capital base once again.

Incidentally, when we look at the United States today, we have to say that we are impressed by the speed at which this three-step plan is being implemented. First the US$ has collapsed to the point where Brazilian super-models will no longer accept to be paid in what was once the defining currency of, if not the world, at least all of the American continent! Secondly, US banks (whether Citigroup, Morgan Stanley, Merrill Lynch…) have put up their hands and offered equity at preferential terms to recapitalize their balance sheets extremely quickly and the weekest links (ie.: Bear Stearns, Countrywide) have been absorbed by stronger players. And thirdly, the Fed is rapidly collapsing interest rates to bring about a mildly steep yield curve.

So does all this mean that the US will be out of the woods in no time? Maybe not. Over the years, we have had the chance to witness several bubbles come and go. And, while it is obvious that two bubbles are never the same, it seems that bubbles often show similar patterns. In fact, we find two different kinds of bubbles. The first kind of bubble takes place on non-productive assets (typically land & real estate, but also tulips, or gold…). The second kind of bubble takes place on productive assets (canals, railroads, telecom lines). In the first kind of bubble, prices are bid higher due to a 'rarity' factor. In the second kind of bubble, prices rise because investors misjudge the future returns of the assets. When the bubbles burst, in the first case, we are left with no more land (or gold, or oil…) then what we started with. In the second case, productive capital has been put in place which can still be exploited, either by its current owners, or by a new set of owners.

An example of the first kind of bubble would be the tulip-mania of 18th century Holland. An example of the second is the US and UK railway bubble of the 19th century or the tech and telecom bubble of the late 1990s. In Holland, when the tulip bubble burst, people were left with their eyes to cry with. In the US and the UK, when the railway bubble burst, the domestic economies still had trains to ride. All around the world, when the telecom bubble burst, consumers were left with the ability to make cheaper calls and transfer more data at a lower cost. In turn, this led to much higher levels of productivity (i.e., the birth of Indian and Filipino call centers), growth and a higher standard of living.

Another very important difference between bubbles is in the way that they are financed:

1. If the bubble is financed by banks, when the bubble bursts, the banks' capital disappears and the velocity of money collapses (for more on velocity, see *Our Brave New World*).

2. If the bubble is financed by capital markets (corporate bonds, junk bonds and equities…), those owning the overvalued assets take a beating.

If they hold those assets on leverage, then the assets get transferred to more financially sound owners. Otherwise, the buck stops with the overpriced assets' owners.

So the worst possible bubble (i.e., the most recessionary) is a bubble in unproductive assets (gold, land, tulips...) financed by banks. The best possible kind of bubble (i.e., one that does not hurt growth too badly) is a bubble in productive assets, financed by capital markets.

The Japanese bubble of the late 1980's was a 'bad' bubble. It was mostly in real estate and was financed by Japanese banks. By contrast, the bubble of the late 1990's was a 'good' bubble. It was mostly in technology (too much telecom and computing expansion) and was financed by capital markets (junk bonds and equities).

Then there is one last differentiating factor between bubbles, namely the policy response and the ability of companies to go bankrupt. Indeed, in order for deflation to end, **productive assets have to move from weak hands to strong hands**. But unfortunately, this does not happen so easily. For assets to move from weak hands to strong hands, one needs to have in place the following very important elements:

- A willingness from policy-makers to allow companies to go bankrupt, regardless of the impact on local employment.

- Bankruptcy laws which permit creditors to gain control of underperforming assets and restructure companies.

- Efficient markets which permit the transfers of underperforming assets from weak hands to strong hands.

If the above factors are not in place, then inefficient companies continue to live on. They become 'zombie companies', waste capital (whether human or financial), drag down the returns on invested capital for competitors, maintain excess capacity in the system, and keep prices low for everyone. This of course has been the main problem of Japan since its bubble burst in 1990. It is for this very reason that my colleague

Alfred Ho always tells me: "Remember Louis, the Japanese can produce anything, but a profit". This inability to transfer assets from "weak hands" to "strong hands" is one of the explanations why Japan is still mired in a deflationary bust, while the US economy barely shrank as it adapted to a post-tech bubble world.

But going back to our current problem, namely the US housing bubble and its aftermath, here is what we do know:

- The US housing bubble was mostly the "worst kind" of bubble. It was a bubble on unproductive goods (mostly houses in lower middle-class neighbourhoods, secondary homes in Florida or Arizona, etc…), financed by excessive bank lending.

- Fortunately, unlike other countries, the US is rather efficient at dealing with its financial problems. We are thus witnessing a rapid pace of recapitalization of banks and financial companies that is nothing short of baffling.

- The US is also rather efficient at moving assets from "weak hands" to "strong hands". One of the problems today, however, is that the "strong hands" often happen to be somewhat brown, or yellow-skinned!

Indeed a decade ago, most of the world's savings resided in the OECD. Within the OECD, these savings were usually managed by private (i.e.: Fidelity, Capital Research, Axa, Harvard Endowment…) or semi-private (i.e.: Calpers, Caisse des Depots…) shareholder-value maximising entities. But today, the picture is a lot more confusing.

For a start, a growing pool of the world's savings are no longer in the OECD but instead in Asia, Russia, or the Middle-East. Secondly, these savings are often not in private hands, but instead in very public institutions. Of course, some of this is not new. ADIA, the GIC or the Kuwait Investment Fund have been around for at least a generation. And by and large, their investments in Western companies have triggered no protectionist backlash. Of course, this may be because no one feels threatened by Kuwait, Abu Dhabi or Singapore.

But can the same be said of China, Russia, or even South Korea? What will happen if, tomorrow, Russia decides to buy 10% of EADS and requests a seat on the board? Or if China wants to purchase 25% of Morgan Stanley? Or if South Korea accumulates a position in Toyota or Volkswagen? Will the various OECD countries accept the presence of shareholders on their boards whose main concerns may not be shareholder value maximisation?

Let us make no mistake about it: with the recent flurry of activity from the world's new Sovereign Wealth Funds, China, Russia, and the greater Middle East are now saying in unison to the OECD: "We are no longer interested in accumulating your debt; we now want a piece of the action." But how will OECD countries react? Right now, we are in a situation of "beggars can't be choosers" and politicians are by and large relieved to see China and the Gulf states recapitalize our bust banking systems.

In fact, in that respect, it could be argued that the credit crunch came just in time to derail what seemed to be growing protectionist tendencies in the halls of US & EU power. Indeed, a few months ago, it seemed as if rich countries were preparing efforts to prevent inflows of direct investment by firms from "undesirable" countries such as China, Russia, and Middle Eastern oil autocracies.

The reality of course is that the generation of immense–and apparently long-lasting–current account surpluses in these "undesirable" countries means that large flows of direct investment from them to the rich countries are inevitable. Still flickers of resistance had started to spring up in the US. First, in 2005, came the vitriolic Congressional reaction to Chinese oil firm CNOOC's proposed takeover of Unocal (which was scuttled) and the acquisition of US port assets by Dubai Ports via its purchase of P&O (which resulted in a divestiture of said assets).

July 2007 saw a potentially ominous development of this theme: the passage of legislation strengthening the Committee on Foreign Investment in the United States (CFIUS). CFIUS, which is charged with evaluating the national-security impact of foreign investments in the US, was set up in 1988 in reaction to a flood of Japanese investment; the Japanese tide receded soon thereafter, and the committee fell into obscurity. The new legislation brought the committee back to life by widening the scope of its reviews to include major energy assets and any systems and assets, whether virtual or physical deemed vital to US national security. A CFIUS review cannot block a transaction, but it can make life so difficult for the parties that they may prefer to give up.

Americans in the 1980s hated the idea of a Japanese takeover, but grew quite content in the 1990s with the reality of Japanese-owned car plants. CNOOC was pushed away from Unocal, which had virtually no US retail presence; but Russia's Lukoil bought up second-tier oil company Getty and has now put its own name on all the old Getty gas stations, with no apparent consumer backlash. It may be that, after a decade or so of getting used to the idea, Americans are now able to put up with Chinese and Arab investment as well? If this ends up being one of the legacies of the credit crunch, then at least all the pain and suffering will not have been for naught... Capitalism's invisible hand sometimes works in mysterious ways.

A Typical Supply-Side Cycle?

When we launched GaveKal in the fall of 1998, we attempted to build our theoretical framework of the world we live in and wrote the following piece which we sent to all three of our then existing clients (Alliance Capital, Marshall-Wace, GIC). The piece was an attempt to identify the kinds of crises the various economies around the world were going through as, even back then, we felt that "things were different this time". In light of what has happened in the US in the past six months, we thought that reproducing this piece would be of interest to the reader. The piece pretty much reads as it should except for one big change: where we say "Asia" (remember this was 1998!) our reader should now input "USA", and vice versa!

"The long debacle in Japan, followed by the collapse in the rest of Asia, has been widely covered by a number of excellent commentators. But even for the casual observer there is the strong feeling that the mechanics of the Asians bear markets have been totally different from those of the post World War II bear markets. The Japanese and the Asian problems have very little in common with the troubles experienced in the Keynesian, inflationary world of 1945 to 1990. We are facing a new animal: the very nature of the economic system has changed. Our goal is thus to rebuild our understanding of this new (or is it old?) environment...

A. A reminder: the "demand-led" economy

The demand-led economy was characterised by excess demand more or less all the time. This excess demand found its sources in an ever-present budget deficit which *more often than not, was monetized by a central bank very seldom independent from the political powers. In such an economy, the **analysis of liquidity is essential.***

In an excess-demand economy, the bear market in financial assets takes place during the "liquidity crisis" phase of the cycle. During those periods we have a contraction of money supply in real terms, an inverted yield curve, a fall in financial assets, and a positive correlation between the bond and the stock markets. The currency is weak entering into the liquidity crisis and strengthens only when short rates are high enough to insure a recession and an improvement in external trade.

B. The new (maybe old) supply-led economy, in force from the beginning of capitalism to 1945, and from 1990 to...?

The economy is led by capital spending. New inventions and new territories create a double impetus: the capacity to satisfy the demand for the new products (or to develop the new territories) has to be built together with the capacity needed to create from scratch such a new stock of capital. As long as the return on invested capital is perceived to be higher than the cost of money, there is no problem in the system...

However, there comes a time when the returns on investments fall below the cost of money. Sales start falling in the capital goods sector and/or in real estate. Needless to say, given the long delays, the momentum in the capital spending sector does not stop immediately and as such overcapacity is created.

Given that large proportions of these investments have been financed by what was known in the past as "an inflation of debt", we run into a debt crisis. The creditors are alarmed and try to call in their loans; as a result money supplies shrinks. Banks go bankrupt. The price level goes down. The weight of the debt in real terms goes up faster than the repayments can be made. More bankruptcies follow. In such a world, happiness is a positive cash flow...

In summary, the economies move in three phases:

* *The asset price inflation*

- *The crisis*

- *The debt deflation.*

The asset inflation *(or debt inflation) part of the cycle always takes place with the assertion that "this time it is different", which for most of the period is true. In the upswing we always find two components: the belief in a new paradigm and the use of financial leverage. Indeed, the excess returns earned on assets acquired through leveraging lead eventually to a massive increase in borrowing, and later on to overcapacity.*

The crisis *occurs when most of the market participants suddenly realize that the cost of money is now higher than the return on invested capital. Usually the crisis is very short. It was called by the economists of those periods "a panic". The chief result of the panic is to change massively the relative prices of assets between the new paradigm sectors and the rest of the economy.*

The debt deflation *can then start: the cost of money moves even higher above the return on invested capital. The prices of assets put as collateral on loans collapse. Bankruptcies and bank failures multiply. The money supplies contract. Prices fall across the board. Real interest rates go up, leading to more bankruptcies…*

The end of the process takes place when the productive assets have moved from financially weak to financially strong owners. The rate of return on invested capital moves above the interest rates (at a very low nominal level). The next cycle can begin.

Three characteristics of this supply-led cycle must be mentioned.

- *In the past, the cycle took roughly ten years to unfold (Juglar).*

- *The downswing (in today's language, the recession) was much longer than the post-1945, post Keynes, recessions (roughly twice as long).*

- *The general price level did not change from the beginning of the crisis to the next crisis or from the beginning of the upswing to the end of the downswing. Price variations occurred in the asset markets, not in the general price level.*

The financial implications of a supply-led cycle are quite straightforward:

In the upswing, interest rates rise and so does the stock market. During the panic, interest rate differentials between high-quality and low-quality borrowers widen dramatically. The stock market tumbles. In the downswing interest rates decline, but the demand for credit keeps falling. The stock market moves sideways at best, in a very wide trading range, which stays in place for at least four or five years. In other words, shares and high-quality bonds are negatively correlated: shares and low quality bonds outperform cash and investment grade bonds in the upswing. In the downswing and in the panic the reverse is true.

In the expansionary phase there is a massive creation of wealth. In the contraction there is a shift in the ownership of productive assets. In the upswing, entrepreneurs get rich. In the downswing the well-capitalised financiers cash in.

To quote Galbraith, is a financial genius somebody who buys when it's going up and has no memory, or is a financial genius somebody who has a lot of cash at the end of a bear market? Today, the financial geniuses in the US or in Asia are of a very different type…

C. A micro-economic view on elasticity

*A good, or a service, is deemed to be **elastic to prices** if a fall in prices is more than compensated for by an increase in revenues (sales). An elasticity above one means that a fall in price increases revenues whilst an elasticity below one means that a fall in prices leads to a fall in revenues.*

*A good or a service is deemed to be **elastic to revenues** if a rise in a population's disposable income leads to a rise in sales (i.e.: luxury goods, tourism etc…). Inelasticity to revenues means that a variation in consumer income has little impact on a product's sales (i.e.: tobacco, food…).*

If we combine these two notions we can see that there are four possible combinations for a given good or service:

1. ***Elastic to price & elastic to revenues:*** *telecoms, computers, tourism…*

2. ***Inelastic to price & elastic to revenues:*** *luxury goods, real estate…*

3. ***Inelastic to price & inelastic to revenues:*** *food, tobacco…*

4. ***Elastic to price & inelastic to revenues:*** *electricity, energy…*

*In a supply led cycle, growth comes from the goods that are **elastic to prices and elastic to revenues:** prices falling in these sectors lead automatically to a big increase in the volume of production and to a significant rise in employment (revenues going up). This, in turn, allows more people to buy the goods, which allows for further declines in prices and greater increases in volumes…*

However, one day the decline in prices is not compensated by an increase in sales, or an increase in disposable income. Or, alternatively, an increase in disposable income does not lead to higher sales. Overcapacity sets in. The return on invested capital falls far below expectations.

A consolidation of the sectors, which used to be the growth sectors then takes place and we move towards a mature market. Very mature markets (scenario number 3) are profoundly indifferent to disposable income and prices. The demand is led solely by the replacement of existing units.

D. Micro, macro & financial markets

If we try to link the macro and the microeconomic views, then we can perhaps advance the following ideas:

- *The upswing takes place when, at the margin, the goods produced have a high elasticity to prices or a high elasticity to rising revenues. In other words, the growth in the economy is led by the high elasticity sectors. It should be noted here that it also means that the forecasting or the measuring of this growth is very difficult: the statistical apparatus almost by definition measures the low elasticity, mature sectors. The only coincident indicator that one can use is employment (which will be a lagging indicator in the downswing).*

- *The fall in elasticity typical of scenario 2 or 4 leads to the **panic**. The panic is nothing but an effort by the markets to adjust the asset prices to the new environment. The adjustment can be very, very fast as everybody realises at the same time that the expected returns will not materialise anymore...*

- *Eventually, we reach scenario number 3 where replacement demand is the main force in the economy (stable part of the downswing).*

Needless to say, at any given point in time, we have all four scenarios coexisting in the same economy. What matters is of course the relative weight of each sector and its contribution to employment and growth.

If one accepts this analysis, then one should invest in "stocks involved in the growth process" of scenario number 1. On arrival into scenario 3, one should go for "value investing". At the same time, the uncertainties of scenario 2 and 4 should lead the money manager to the greatest possible caution. It is advisable to diversify portfolios using high-quality bonds.

*A practical point should be made here: **when a panic starts, one has plenty of time to start "buying on dips"; in fact such a strategy is typically a scenario 1 strategy**, (as evidenced by the plight of the Asians markets).*

As far as currencies are concerned, in a global economy, one of the main determinants of the cost of capital for a given country is the capital flows emanating from other parts of the world (e.g. the capital flows to Asia from 1990 to 1996). As such, the real exchange rate of a currency goes UP in scenario 1 as investors want to participate in the extraordinary returns available.

The low price of money supports the capital- spending boom and creates the conditions for a current account deficit. Eventually the exchange rate becomes overvalued and the return on invested capital, on average, falls to a more normal level, through a decline in the profitability of the sectors exposed to outside competition. As long as the dominant sectors pull the economy, the danger is small of a massive decline in the exchange rate. It is only when those aforementioned sectors peak that the exchange rate is in trouble. Part of the asset price adjustment will then take place through the exchange rate.

This brings us to a second practical remark: **when the panic arrives, one should expect to lose money not only on financial assets but also on the currency in which those assets are denominated (as Asia has shown).**

And this takes us to our third asset class, the bond market. In the upswing the name of the game is to have an equity portfolio invested in the dominant sectors. At that time, who needs the bond market?

However, when the panic hits, the best diversification is probably in high-quality foreign bonds: the fall in the demand for capital leads to a worldwide decline in nominal interest rates and the decline in the exchange rate boosts the return available in foreign bonds…

E. Conclusion

In the inflationary, Keynesian world, the economic and financial system does not change in nature from the beginning to the end of the cycle. In a supply-led deflationary world we have two very distinctive parts, the upswing and the downswing.

In the upswing, the stock market goes up, interest rates go up, employment goes up, and bank shares outperform. One has to be a "growth stock manager" while the main investment decision tools have to be built around the notion of **momentum** *(earnings momentum, share price momentum, sales momentum).*

In the downswing, the stock market is either flat or down, high-quality bonds go up, money supply goes down, and credit is cheap but not available. The main investment philosophy to follow is value-oriented (Graham-Dodd). **Balance sheet analysis becomes absolutely crucial.**

Our big surprise in the last two years has been to see one-third of the world in a deflationary bust and two-thirds in a deflationary boom. Naively, we thought that we should have had the same dominant environment everywhere. The question that we have now in our mind is: can this dichotomy be maintained?"

Ten years later, investors have to ask themselves exactly the same question but in reverse: can one part of the world (Asia, Middle-East, Latin America, Africa…) boom while another part of the world busts (Europe, USA…)? And this question brings us to our second, and probably most important, revolutionary mega-trend, namely the rise of the emerging markets.

The Rise of the Emerging Markets–Using China as an Example

In the early 1990s, as I was set to start university, my father went on a two-week business trip around China. When he came back, he told me: "You have to learn Chinese, because China will become very important for the global economy. Moreover, no one there speaks English." My father's advice demonstrated a fair amount of vision. And it also showed his natural inclination to get any heavy lifting done by somebody else. Indeed, Charles did not come back from China thinking "I have to learn Chinese" but instead "I should get Louis to learn Chinese".

Studying Chinese was, it turned out, no walk in the park. It was time and labor intensive. And as a result I was never very good at it - even after spending eight months in China in the mid 1990s studying at Nanjing University, my Mandarin remained very weak.

Fortunately, Charles was right: China's economy did wonders and helped justify the time spent on the language books and character cards. Better yet, the Chinese economy opened so rapidly that, in the spate of a few years, a large number of individuals in China had learnt to speak English (contrary to what my father had experienced). This allowed me to put the Chinese language books away and concentrate on the more exciting bit: the economic success story which allowed for hundreds of millions of people to move from near-starvation to middle-class in a little over a generation.

Unfortunately, my years spent studying and focusing on China mean that I feel more comfortable talking about this growing giant than the other economic success stories of the past few years (Brazil, Russia, India, Vietnam…). As such, I hope that my readers will forgive the fact that most of the examples I use to talk about the exciting growth of the emerging markets are more focused on China than any other country.

The fact that I have spent a lot of time reading about China over the past decade does not, of course, prevent me from sometimes saying really stupid things. A case in point was our core thesis in *Our Brave New World*. In that book, we tried to show that, as Western economies evolved from being industrial-based to being service-based, the volatility of growth collapsed. The sharp reduction in the volatility of growth then helped explain some of the events witnessed in recent years such as the stronger willingness of consumers to leverage, the rise in asset prices, the so-called unsustainable trade deficit, etc…).

In *Our Brave New World* we also wrote: "*We have argued that the volatility of the US economy is contracting because US companies are increasingly sending the low-value added, high fixed costs part of their production process abroad. But if the US is exporting its volatility, it means that someone is importing it. This someone is usually in an 'emerging market' (China, Mexico, Brazil, South Korea…). In turn, this means that, while the US worker is less likely to be fired at the bottom of the cycle (which allows him to take on more leverage), the Emerging Market consumer is more likely to get fired when times get lean. Which means that, while the income of the Emerging Market consumer is rising fast, so is the volatility of that income*" (Chapter 7).

That was stupid. It was a typical case of non-sequitur logic. Or worse yet, it was a case of looking at Emerging Markets through our Western World prism.

On the volatility scale, an economy can do much worse than be industrial-based: it can be agricultural-based and thus at the mercy of the elements. Take the US as an example: one hundred fifty years ago, if hale storms destroyed the harvest, and agricultural output fell, it made for a serious economic downturn. Today, who monitors, and who cares how much wheat the US produces (apart from the people who trade it)? Simply put, agriculture no longer has an important impact on the overall US economy. And this is a very positive development, for agriculture is the worst of possible businesses. The world's poor farmers simply never know what tomorrow will be made of. Will it rain? Too little? Too much? Will it be too hot? Too cold?

When agriculture is a big part of an economy, then the economy is extremely volatile. Take India (where 65% of people still toil the land for a living) as an example: despite the country's impressive growth, the economic cycle there remains very much tied to the harvests. When harvests are weak, the economy feels the pinch. And when the harvests are strong, the economy booms.

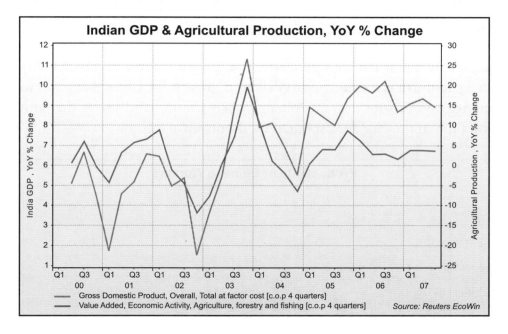

Or take China: until recently, half of Chinese workers were farmers.

This high percentage of Chinese workers involved in farming could be considered a source of concern (i.e.: low disposable income, strong sensitivity of earnings to unforeseeable events, etc...). But that would be a "glass half empty" type of approach. For the other side of the

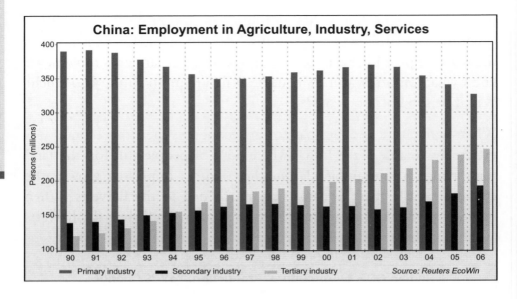

China: Employment in Agriculture, Industry, Services

Primary industry   Secondary industry   Tertiary industry   Source: Reuters EcoWin

argument is that **the high percentage of the labor force involved today in agriculture is a tremendous driver of growth for China for years to come.** And this for a simple reason: when a farm hand leaves the farm for a job in the city, his productivity shoots up.

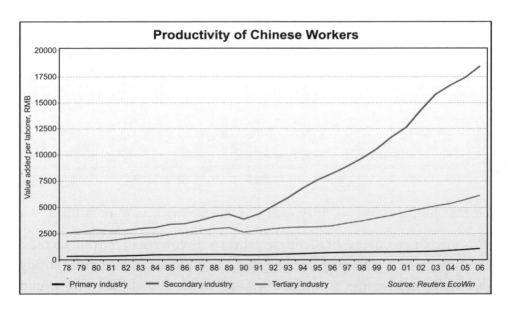

Productivity of Chinese Workers

Primary industry   Secondary industry   Tertiary industry   Source: Reuters EcoWin

In 2004, average annual returns to labor in agriculture in China were US$300; in services US$900, and in industry, US$3,000. Enormous gains in China have thus been made, and will continue to be achieved, simply by moving workers from farms into urban occupations.

One of the most important components of China's impressive economic growth of the past quarter century (9.4% average annual real GDP growth between 1980-2004, by official figures) is the immense productivity gains arising from the shift of labor from low-productivity agriculture to higher-productivity services and industry. Of course, this simple fact immediately raises the question of whether China will be able to continue shifting unproductive labour from the countryside to the cities? And the answer to this question is an unequivocal Yes!

Looking ahead at the next twenty years, one of the surer trends we can count on is that a growing number of Chinese workers will leave the countryside (for reasons we plan to go into later in the book, but which include the desertification and environmental devastation of large parts

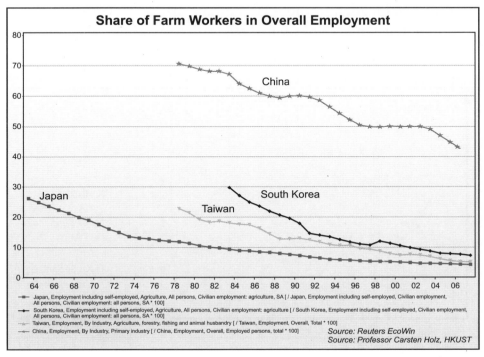

of the countryside, the growth in wages in manufacturing and services, the growth in education, etc...) to move into cities. And as this happens, we should witness the same effects that we saw in Japan, Taiwan or South Korea a few decades ago: big productivity gains and accelerating growth. As China continues to 'waste' less human capital in its fields, growth will remain solid.

And the positive effects of China's "de-agriculturalization" do not stop at the productivity gains. For a start, when a country moves from agriculture to industry, the volatility of its cycle falls; which is why we were wrong when we wrote in *Our Brave New World* that volatility in the emerging markets should rise–it should fall, as agriculture becomes an ever-shrinking part of GDP. Looking at global GDP, a few things jump out at us, namely that:

- Services are an ever growing part of the global economy; and

- Agriculture is an ever-shrinking part of the global economy

And the combination of those facts means that the volatility of global growth, not just in developed markets, is set to continue falling (barring any major policy mistakes).

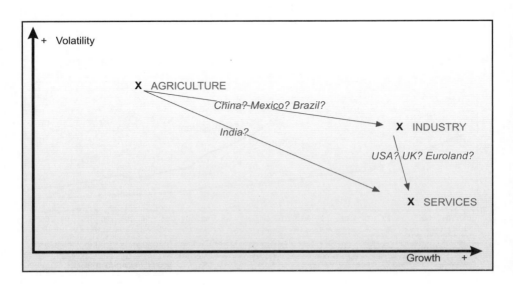

This is of course very true for China. **As the percentage of people working in agriculture falls, China will not only continue to register impressive productivity gains, but will also continue to see sharp falls in the volatility of its economic growth** (since services/industry are less cyclical than agriculture).

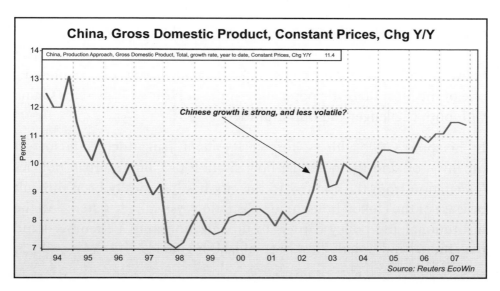

Another secondary impact of the move away from agriculture and towards industry and services is a large boost in consumption. Indeed, even at equal annual revenues, a farmer and a factory worker will tend to display very different consumption patterns. The farmer who earns 100 will tend to spend 50 and save 50. Why? For a start, on a farm, one can live in a very autarkical way. But more importantly, since farming is such an unreliable and unpredictable business, farmers always have to save for a "non-rainy" day.... If there is no rain tomorrow, they don't eat! By contrast, the factory worker, and to an even greater extent, the service worker, usually feels pretty confident that his job will still be there in a month's time. So his natural inclination is to take his paycheck to the bank and say: "Look, I earn 100 a month. Can you lend me 500 to buy a motorcycle and I'll pay you back over the next three years?" And of course, the bank can do that for the worker (in a way that it can not for the farmer), since this is a regular cash-flow that can be projected into the future.

So along with higher productivity, and less volatility, the change from farm hand to factory worker also implies a much stronger rate of consumption, and a lower savings rate.

Over the past decade, China's cities have added approximately 100 million people. Over the next ten years, estimates range from anywhere between 150m to 300m people! Such a rapid urbanisation represents one of the most dramatic population shifts in History. It presents China with both challenges and opportunities.

In his final CCP address, former President Jiang focused a lot on urbanisation and the potential liberalisation of China's urban policies (emigration from the country to the city has historically been difficult because of the Hukou household registration system). He stated: "All the institutional and policy barriers to urbanization must be removed and the rational and orderly flow of rural labour guided."

The current deregulation of the housing/registration policy is unleashing a new wave of growth around China. This presents both opportunities and huge challenges for the Chinese government. After all, China's urban migration requires massive capital spending: housing, schools, sewer systems, power plants, transport systems... all of which need to be built if China is to avoid its cities spurring shanty-towns such as Cairo, Lagos, Calcutta etc... So far, the government has mostly responded by accelerating deregulation (i.e., home ownership schemes, growth of mortgage industry, deregulation of the utilities industries, relaxation of foreign-ownership rules on logistic and transport companies, recapitalization of banks, privatisation of property...).

Around 80% of China's growth in the past ten years has come from its cities. Over that period of time, China has added nearly 200 'new' cities. We can probably expect this pattern to continue for the next decade and then some...

One last, important but rarely talked about, consequence of urbanisation: it brings women into the workforce in ever greater numbers. This can be a major boon to productivity, but also has other implications, most importantly a serious fall in birth rates (more on that later).

Signs of Progress-Tourism & Education

One of the most frequent questions I receive from clients is: "How reliable is Chinese data?" This is a great question, for it has a simple, straightforward answer: not at all. Indeed, the inadequacies of China's statistical releases are so well documented that it is not that worthwhile to dwell further into it. Nevertheless, despite the imperfect nature of Chinese data, you will find a fair amount of it scattered around in this book, usually in the aim to prove various theories. This reflects the fact that:

- Like Keynes said, "it is better to be approximately right, than precisely wrong".

- Though Chinese data in and of itself might not be very reliable, information can sometimes be detected in changes in the data.

- Not all the data is massively flawed, and some of the statistics are actually enlightening.

- Everyone else throws the Chinese statistics around... so why wouldn't we?

- And finally, like Churchill said, "Most economists use statistics like a drunk uses a lamp-post; for support, not for light."

Having said that, whatever statistics one wants to use to measure the emergence of China (i.e.: adjusted for purchasing parity differences, it is now the second largest economy in the World), one thing is obvious to even the most casual visitor to Beijing, Shanghai or elsewhere in the Middle Kingdom: China is a country on the move. Consider the following:

Infant Mortality:

China's infant mortality rate has fallen to about 33 per 1,000, and in large cities, such as Beijing and Shanghai, the infant mortality rate has dropped to 5.05 per 1,000. This China city rate is comparable to the rates achieved in the best First World countries, such as Japan or Sweden where the mortality rate is slightly below 4 per 1,000. But most importantly, it reflects rather favorably when compared against the mortality rates prevalent in the 1950s (at the time of the "Great Leap Forward" and the massive famine that ensued) of 300 per 1,000.

Life Expectancy:

With a life expectancy of over 72 years, people in China can now look forward to nearly as long a life as people in North America or Western Europe. What a difference thirty years have made:

Table 1: Life Expectancy in Different Countries and Regions

	1950-55	1975-80	2002	2006
France	66	74	79	79.7
United Kingdom	69	73	78	78.6
India	39	53	64	54.7
China	41	65	71	72.6
Africa	38	48	50	NA
World	46	60	67	NA

Source: CIA Factbook

Literacy:

Still according to the CIA factbook, 90.9% of Chinese people today can read and write. This is an impressive, and important, feat given the fact that:

- A couple of generations ago, only a minority of scholars could read and write

- Chinese characters help tie the nation together. Indeed, while people all across the land speak different dialects (though all radio and TV media, as well as school curriculums, are in Mandarin), people who speak different dialects can always communicate with each other by writing, since the characters always mean the same words (it is their pronunciation which differs).

- Learning to read and write Chinese is a really strenuous exercise (trust me, I tried!).

We could continue to rattle off numbers highlighting China's growth of recent years and thereby numb our reader to sleep. Or we could illustrate

what China's economic growth concretely means. If, as Napoleon said, a picture is worth a thousand words, then the picture on the previous page, illustrates accurately what is happening in China today.

The picture, taken on a weekend in the coastal city of Qingdao (most famous for its Tsingtao beer), illustrates a simple fact: an increasing number of Chinese are wealthy enough to take time off from the daily grind of earning a living and are thus able to "relax" at the beach. More than anything, the growth in Chinese tourism, and the fact that even Germans would be incapable of finding a spot for their towels on a Chinese beach, illustrate **how far China has come over the past decades.**

Some of our Calvinist readers might take us to task for creating an analogy between tourism/taking leisure time and progress. It could indeed probably be argued that taking the approach that people work to: Sustain themselves and then Enjoy the fruits of their labor by sitting on an overly crowded beach is a very European approach to the question of why people work.

But, perhaps reflecting our cultural biases, it is an approach we believe to be valid. And we thus see the rise in China's tourist industry as a phenomenal example of how far the country has come... and how much more ground it will soon be covering.

Consider the following: in 1997, Japanese outward tourism reached a peak with 17m Yen-rich, Nikon-toting Japanese going overseas. That same year, the Chinese government for the first time allowed its citizens to travel for leisure abroad. **By 2003, in just six years, China overtook Japan as Asia's biggest supplier of outbound travelers. In 2004, nearly 29m Chinese traveled abroad.** A bullish World Tourism Organization (WTO) predicts that China will be the major growth engine of world outbound tourism over the next 15 years. **It estimates 50m Chinese will go abroad by 2010, rising to 100m by 2020.**

So if you think the growth of China will not impact your daily life, you are most likely wrong: on your next holiday to Paris/London/New York, on your visit to the Louvre/Tate/Met, you are likely to find yourself behind a long queue of Chinese tourists....

Table 2: Value of total personal travel and tourism sector by country, 2005, US $ bn

2005		2015 forecast	
United States	883.3	United States	1,633.80
Japan	286.8	Japan	382.9
Germany	196.1	China	306.5
United Kingdom	194.9	United Kingdom	252.2
France	155.6	Germany	214.6
Italy	125.4	France	195.5
Spain	125.4	Italy	159.9
China	89.9	Spain	131.9
Canada	78.6	Canada	108.5
Mexico	57.7	Mexico	96.5

Source: World Travel & Tourism Council Oxford Economic Forecasting

Hence follows our first piece of advice: do any bit of tourism you have wanted to do for a while as soon as possible, because in the near future, the place you wanted to visit (provided it is a major destination) will be rather crowded. And of course, this goes double for China's grand sites (The Forbidden City, the Great Wall, the Summer Palace, the Temple of Heaven, the Jiuzhaigou National Park, Huangshan, Emeishan, Guilin/Yangshuo, Lijiang, Xian…). Already these places, on a busy day, tend to look like the aforementioned beach.

The message is simple enough: putting a number on China's progress over the past decade is a futile exercise. **But one thing is certain: an ever-increasing number of people in China live better, longer and more stimulating lives than their parents did.** In fact, for the first time in its history, China can stop looking at the past and pretend that it once lived in a "Golden Age" to which everyone should aspire to return (one of the very core principles of Confucianism). In casual conversations with people in China, most seem to agree that things have never been this good. A country which knew nothing but misery, humiliation, devastation, war, repression and famine for a hundred years between the Opium Wars and the death of Mao is now full of hope, and pride. As China makes a grand entrance into *Our Brave New World*, it is a very exciting place to be.

Beyond tourism, another sign of the progress unfolding across the Middle Kingdom is the sheer explosion in higher education. As I write, China now has more people enrolled in university than the US. This means that, from practically nowhere ten years ago, China is now in a situation where, in a few years, **it will produce more university graduates than any other country.**

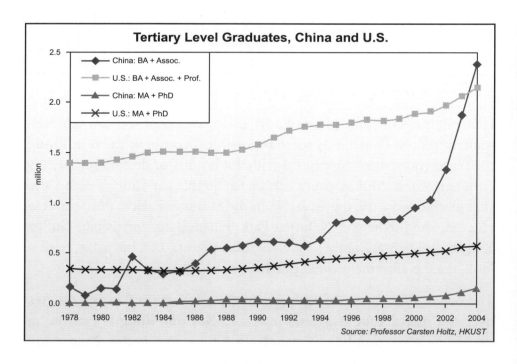

Source: Professor Carsten Holtz, HKUST

To be sure, one might argue that Chinese universities do not offer the same level of education as American universities. But that would be missing the point for three reasons:

1. Even an "inferior" education is much better than no education at all. So, if nothing else, the spike in education over the past five years represents a huge progress from where China was just a few years ago.

2. While the top Chinese universities cannot rival the top US universities, the average Chinese university is probably as good as the average US community college/small state school.

3. Along with the growth in enrollment in domestic universities, we have also witnessed a large growth in Chinese students leaving to study in the world's top universities (Harvard, Yale, Oxford...). In 2004, more than 114,600 Chinese students went abroad to study (according to statistics from China's education ministry). So the very best in China do get top-notch educations.... And some do come back. In the last five years, the number of Chinese returning from overseas stints has been increasing every year, exceeding 25,000 in 2007.

The Chinese government has an ambitious set of 50-year educational targets, and many of the intermediate milestones are well on their way to being met (it is, however, important to note that the government has not provided a convincing mechanism for financing its more ambitious educational aims).

As a result, when the pace of productivity gains from sheer workforce transformation from agriculture to services and industry (as described in the previous chapter) begins to fall, productivity gains from higher levels of education should pick up the slack.

The first, and most obvious place, the rapid pace of China's educational gains can best be assessed is in the impressive progress of young people's knowledge of English. As mentioned above, while ten years ago staff at hotels, airport counters and the like barely had any knowledge of English, today, in big cities, a Chinese person fluent in English never seems to be far away (and willing to help).

China's key education objectives, 2001-2050

Objective	2001	2010	2020	2050
Population receiving 9-year compulsory education, %	85	95	99	-
Gross senior secondary school enrollment rate, %	54	73	85	100
Gross tertiary enrollment rate, %	13	23	40	55
Average years of education of working age population	8.0	9.6	10.0	13.5
Working-age people with higher education, %	4.7	10.5	19.3	44.0
Engineers and scientists per m population	na	na	1,500	3,000
Education expenditure as % of GDP	2.9	6.6	7.2	7.8

Source: China Ministry of Education

A few examples to illustrate the progress made on the language front:

- China already has the world's largest number of people learning English

- English texts are now the fastest growing sector in China's book education market

- **English texts already account for up to 8% of the Chinese retail book market**

This impressive growth has of course not gone unnoticed: Gordon Brown, the UK Prime Minister, said during a recent trip to China that Britain's education exports were now the fastest growing export category, having nearly doubled in five years to £10.3bn. This is equivalent to about 1% of the country's gross domestic product. Mr Brown further said that education exports would be vital to the UK economy - possibly reaching £20bn a year in 15 years' time - and that China is expected to be the primary driver of growth. He said: "In 20 years' time, the number of English speakers in China is likely to exceed the number of speakers of English as a first language in all the rest of the world"....

Though that last point may have been political hyperbole, Mr Brown's point is well taken by anyone who has regularly visited China in the past decade: on the education and language fronts, the country is growing by leaps and bounds. If nothing else, this willingness to learn English sets China apart from other Asian economic success stories such as South Korea or Japan.

Privatization & China's Ricardian Growth Spurt

The shift of production from the state to the private sector has also helped China generate massive productivity gains. As everyone knows, in the past twenty years, China has evolved from being a centrally-planned, communist economy to an economy where the tools of production are increasingly privately-owned, and managed. Sometimes even foreign-owned. And it would take a Historical revisionist to argue that managing an economy through a communist plan will end up being more efficient, and productive, than the market's invisible hand. This is an important point to remember when looking at China's impressive growth of the past two decades. In essence, China started from a very low, highly inefficient base. And there are undeniable, massive transitional benefits when moving from an inefficient state-planned economy to a market-oriented economy. Such a transition triggers enormous productivity gains and economic growth.

In China, since 1998, the state sector's share of business output has fallen by 13 percentage points, to 33%, while the domestic private sector's share rose by 10 points, to 45% (foreign enterprises accounted for the rest). Take a wild guess as to which is more productive: is it a) China's state-owned enterprises or b) China's privately-owned or foreign-owned firms?

Believe it or not, the answer is b). Indeed, according to a recent analysis by the OECD, private firms in China consistently enjoy profit ratios four to five percentage points higher than state firms. **Thus the shift of production from state enterprises to private enterprises produces**

a one-off efficiency gain that boosts growth. Fortunately, this shift is likely to continue at a rapid pace for the next four or five years; for example, the government has slowly been privatizing China's banks and insurance companies.

As China becomes less socialist, China's growth becomes stronger. Nothing that surprising here–it simply follows the History of Mankind as anyone can read it. And for our readers who wonder why a capitalist system fosters stronger growth, we would refer to the second chapter of *Our Brave New World :*

"Capitalism find its growth in two very strong forces:

*1. **Growth can come from a rational organisation of talents:** The best expression of this source of growth was given by David Ricardo, in his law of comparative advantages. Even if a surgeon can type faster than his secretary, if cutting flesh is paid more by the hour than typing letters, the surgeon should hire a secretary to do all of his typing, thereby freeing as much time as possible to cut flesh. This argument is of course most often applied to free trade.*

*2. **Growth can come from inventions put in place by entrepreneurs:** Growth triggered by inventions is a totally different kind of growth altogether. A new invention can trigger new demand, lead to new products, new management techniques, new markets. At the same time, inventions can also lead to the collapse of old products or old firms (i.e: with emails and fax-machines, who still uses a telex?). This is the "creative destruction" which Schumpeter described.*

To promote the Ricardian kind of growth, one needs low trade barriers… To promote the Schumpeterian kind of growth, one needs low regulations, low taxes, easy access to capital and, most importantly, the ability and right to fail. These factors have been prevalent, at least across the Western World, for a generation."

Are these factors becoming prevalent across China as well? There is little doubt in our minds that, by privatizing large segments of its economy, Chinese authorities triggered an **unprecedented Ricardian growth**

spurt. But the problem with Ricardian growth is that it is finite. After an economy has been liberalized, after free trade has been allowed to work its magic, after deregulation has allowed businesses to thrive, then the dividends from the Ricardian re-organization have been cashed in. And one then needs Schumpeterian growth to kick in. Which brings us back to China's privatization: in past decades, China has thrived as the weight of government in the overall economy has continuously shrunk. But there comes a time, when China will no longer get massive gains from "rationalizing/privatizing" its economy. All the privatizing that had to be done will have been achieved.

Fortunately, we are nowhere near that point yet and the shift from public to private sector is likely to continue at a rapid pace for at least the next four or five years. China will continue to privatize and deregulate its industries.

Take retail as an example. On March 1st 2006, the central government finally cut some regulatory slack to foreign retailers operating in the mainland. Today, firms operating retail, wholesale, franchising, and commission-based agency services no longer require central approval from the Ministry of Commerce (Mofcom). More significantly, local authorities are now able to grant distribution rights to foreign-invested enterprises which have long been hamstrung by tight regulations that forced them to distribute via state-owned sales companies.

Previously, foreign-owned manufacturers had to obtain approval from Mofcom before distributing and selling goods in the mainland. Retailers like Wal-Mart and Carrefour had officially been limited to 65% ownership of their mainland operations and had to receive approval from Beijing before opening a store. But now, with the loosening of the rules, a flood of new foreign consumer companies have entered the market. And many existing retailers have pushed into second- and third-tier cities. Big players like Wal-Mart and Britain's B&Q now fully control wholesale and distribution. And who wins out? The Chinese consumer of course!

In China, Ricardian growth still has the wind in its sails. The continued growth of China's private sector industry, and the relative downsizing of the state, will remain excellent news for sustained productivity growth for years to come.

The Growth of Networks, Ports, Roads, Telecom Infrastructure...

Beyond the more efficient use of labor, beyond the gains achieved through education, beyond the more efficient use of capital, there is a fourth and final reason which helps explain China's impressive productivity boom: the growth in infrastructure. And, more than anything, this fourth factor sets China apart from any other emerging country.

Intellectual giants such as David Ricardo and Frederic Bastiat have demonstrated so precisely all the advantages that accrue to countries engaged in free trade that we will just assume that the matter is settled and that we need not discuss the benefits of trade. Having said that, to fully capture the benefits of trade, a country obviously needs to have infrastructure in place: roads to move goods around, ports to load and offload stuff, a telecom backbone to ensure communications between suppliers, producers, clients, etc... Infrastructure spending thus has multiple impacts on growth:

First, infrastructure spending creates its own demand (for asphalt, for network switches, for container cranes...). Two decades ago, there were only two cities in China of economic importance: Shanghai and Beijing. So China only really needed one line of communication. Then Guangzhou grew in prominence and this introduction of a third point created two additional lines of communications (e.g.: flights between Beijing and Guangzhou and Shanghai and Guangzhou). The emergence of Tianjin brought the total to six. The growth in Wuhan brought the total to ten... and so forth.

This enumeration could rapidly become tedious if mathematical theory did not offer a formula to explain this relationship: in a world with N centres, **the number of links between the poles is N(N-1)/2.** Excitingly, every day some new pole is added to the Chinese economy (Chongqing? Chengdu? Dalian?…), so the number of lines of communication grows exponentially. The addition of new Chinese cities into the global producing space requires massive capital spending increases in telecoms, airports, aircrafts, harbours, ships, airline pilots, sailors, train mechanics, truck drivers, tourism capacity, etc.…

Secondly, to this effect of the number (N) of poles increasing, and the required boost in capital spending, we must also add the fact that, as people start to move around and exchange ideas, more inventions come to the surface. So not only do we witness an explosion in the number of lines of communication, but, all of a sudden, we witness the emergence of new means of communications. In time, this spurs growth further.

Events like the emergence of the fax, pagers, e-mail, mobile telephones and the Internet are obviously extremely important, and growth-inducing. The fact that China has moved from zero mobile phone subscribers to 500m subscribers, or that China is now the fastest growing market in the world for Internet users, is nothing short of massively bullish. These are extremely important developments which are simply impossible to factor into econometric models or even classical economic analysis. It works as a step function, with strong periods of economic acceleration as new players and new means of communication emerge.

Thirdly, and most importantly, infrastructure spending allows for a more efficient use of capital, land or labor. For example, if the roads are of poor quality (i.e.: India, Indonesia, Vietnam…), then factories are forced to be next to the ports or railway lines (to make sure they get supplied with intermediate goods and ensure they can move their products around). But land and labor next to ports or railway lines might be more expensive. The congregation of industry around ports can also create bottlenecks.…

In the 1950s, in the US, President Eisenhower pushed a plan through Congress (under the pretenses of national security) for a multi-billion dollar inter-state highway system. This highway system is often referred to as one of the main reasons behind the US economic boom of the 1950s and 1960s. The new highways allowed for a more efficient use of labor, and capital, across a country the size of a continent. It also helped unify the country, as people were able to move around more easily, go to college across the land, find work in different states, etc… It allowed for an appreciation in the price of land outside of cities (as people could now commute into work), and it triggered the growth in companies such as Wal-Mart, Coca-Cola, or McDonald's, which could now deliver services and products in a timely and uniform manner across the US.

Interestingly, the Chinese leadership has recently announced plans for road constructions across the country not dissimilar to what the US did in the 1950s. Dragonomics wrote about this very topic in the June 2007 issue of the *China Economic Quarterly:*

"Nothing reflects the Chinese development model more precisely than the country's commitment to building expressways. As the national savings rate increased in the 1980s, making possible high levels of investment, road construction became the defining image of the 1990s. Whether the swathes cut through townships to make way for new rural expressways, or the character chai ("demolition") slapped on the sides of historic properties blocking ring roads in Shanghai, it became clear the government had an asphalt obsession. Combined with port development and power plant construction, the highway boom made China, by the late 1990s, the first third world country to boast first world infrastructure.

It was not a quick policy choice by the central government. Sir Gordon Wu, the pioneer of Guangdong province's joint venture expressways and chairman of infrastructure developer Hopewell Holdings Ltd (HHL), recalls years of effort to persuade Deng Xiaoping and colleagues of the case for expressway construction. "Back in 1980, I was acting like a missionary," he says. "The leadership didn't see the need for highways when most people still couldn't afford bicycles. Why invest in roads for highways when most people still couldn't afford bicycles. Why invest in roads for the bourgeoisie when you could invest in mass transit railways for everyone?" The answer was not to serve the masses, but to serve the cause of economic growth and particularly the burgeoning export economy. Expressways took investors to cheap labour, and goods to ports.

Expressway construction began in 1988–given traction, according to Mr Wu, by the support of the late premier, Zhao Ziyang. Once made, the commitment to highway development was followed through with a vengeance. By the late 1990s the pace of construction appeared reckless, given that many tolled roads were opening to extremely low traffic flows. A CEQ survey of China's new highways at the end of 1997 wondered how the network could be completed given apparently low investment returns. At that point the country had 4,735km of finished expressways; it already seemed like a lot. Yet, by the end of 2004, the stock had grown to 34,000km, ranking second in the world after the US.

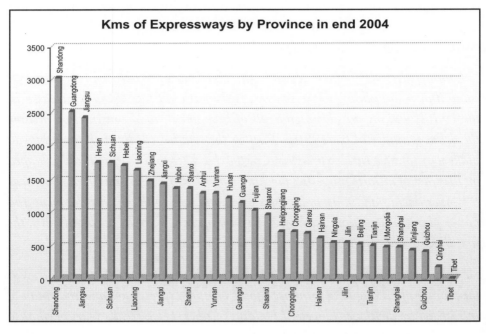

As if to pre-empt speculation that most of its greenfield work is done, the Ministry of Communications, responsible for roads, **published a plan in October to expand the expressway network to 85,000km.** *The blueprint is dubbed "7-9-18", continuing the Chinese love affair with multiple numeric*

targets. **Its basic aim is to connect all towns and cities with a population over 200,000.** *The network will consist of seven expressways radiating from Beijing, nine running from north to south, and 18 crossing from east to west. Trunk roads that link cities will account for 68,000km of the total, while five regional ring roads add a further 17,000km.*

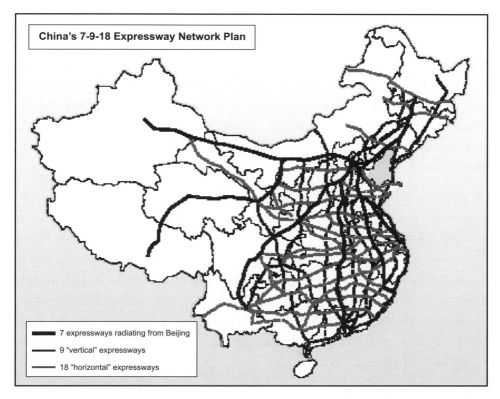

China's 7-9-18 Expressway Network Plan

━━━ 7 expressways radiating from Beijing
─── 9 "vertical" expressways
─── 18 "horizontal" expressways

The total estimated investment over 30 years is Rmb2trn (US$250bn), with an initial annual investment of Rmb140bn-50bn through 2010, **adding approximately 3,000km of road per year.** *While the figures and timetable must be taken with a fistful of salt (one of the expressways runs from Beijing to Taipei!), the government's determination to create a comprehensive expressway network is not in doubt. The past decade proved as much,* **and more than 40% of the network is already complete.** *The new plan expands the original expressway mandate, which focused on an interconnected system along the prosperous east coast. Aside from "beefing up road coverage" in the east, says Minister of Communications Zhang Chunxian, the new target* *is to "interconnect the roads in the central region and realise the accessibility of the expressways in the west".* **On completion, the average resident in eastern provinces should be 30 minutes from the nearest expressway.** *A more significant statistic in terms of the government's agenda to raise the status of inland areas is the aim to provide residents in the central provinces with access to an expressway within one hour, rising to two hours in the remote west."*

There is no doubt in our minds that the feverish road construction currently taking place in China is an extremely bullish development for the country, and for the companies who do business in China. As the road network develops, companies will be able to reach workers and consumers ever further. Both production and distribution costs will plummet.

Another aspect of China's impressive infrastructure boom is the amount of money being spent on building ports. A couple of decades ago, nearly all the Chinese trade with the rest of the World went through Hong Kong (which, as a result, has been amongst the largest ports in the world for some time). But increasingly, Chinese producers, or, as is increasingly the case, international producers with factories in China (foreign firms now account for 56% of China's trade surplus versus just 9% five years ago) are able to bypass Hong Kong and ship straight from Shanghai, Qingdao, Ningbo, Dalian....

Take Shanghai as an example. Shanghai has been the largest port in mainland China for the past five years, and was the third-busiest container port around the world in 2003 and 2004 after Hong Kong and Singapore. In 2004, the ports in Shanghai handled 14.6 million TEUs, up 31% from 11.1 million TEUs in 2003. In value terms, Shanghai registered a 43% YoY increase in total trade value in 2004.

Currently, the two ports in Shanghai (Shanghai Container Terminal-SCT and Waigaoqiao Container Terminal-WCT) are running close to capacity. But, some 90 kilometers away from Shanghai in a place called Yangshan Island, a third group of ports is set to emerge as a dominant player. On

Yanghshan, **the Shanghai government is undertaking the largest port development the world has ever seen.** The total bill? Around US$16 billion (including the 32-km Luyang Bridge).

Upon completion by 2020, the Yangshan port project will consist of 52 berths with a handling capacity of over 30 million TEUs (i.e.: over twice what Shanghai, China's busiest port is handling today). Phase 1 of Yangshan Island, consisting of five berths and with an annual handling capacity of about 3.3 million TEUs, is already completed. The investment in this Phase 1 was about RMB 14.3 billion. Phase 2, consisting of four berths and with an annual capacity of about 2.6 million TEUs, has also just come on stream.

Given the scale of this project, it is hard to see how the government will make money on this investment. But one man's loss is sometimes another man's gain… and with the massive increase in port infrastructure currently underway in China, we can be sure of one thing: the friction costs of shipping stuff to and from China will likely continue to head lower (in 1956 the cost of loading a ship cost US$5.83/ton; today the cost is US$0.16/ton, (thanks, it has to be said to Malcolm McLean's invention of the Twenty Foot Equivalent Unit (TEU) Box).

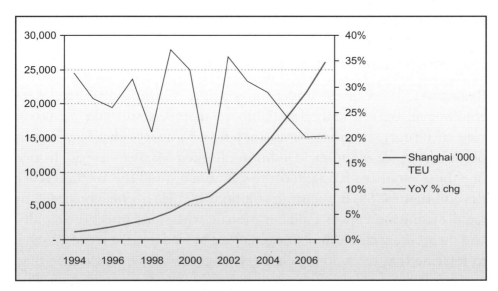

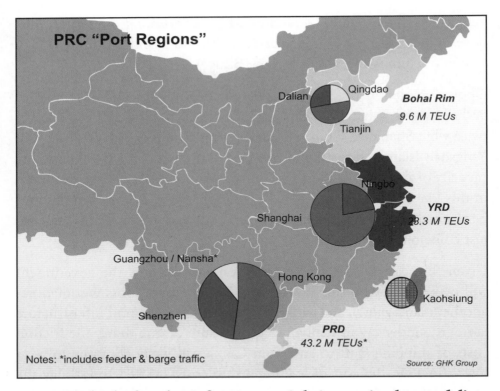

PRC "Port Regions"

Dalian — Qingdao

Bohai Rim
9.6 M TEUs

Tianjin

Ningbo

YRD
28.3 M TEUs

Shanghai

Guangzhou / Nansha*

Hong Kong

Kaohsiung

Shenzhen

PRD
*43.2 M TEUs**

Notes: *includes feeder & barge traffic

Source: GHK Group

Interestingly, the fact that infrastructure is being put in place to deliver and receive goods and services from ever further afield could end up having important macroeconomic/policy consequences. Indeed, one of the recurrent concerns of the Chinese government is inflation, especially food price inflation. Why is the leadership so concerned about food price inflation? For two very simple reasons:

Reason #1: The Chinese leadership might no longer look, or feel, very communist, but a number of Politburo members still take a Marxist view of History. In other words, they tend to believe that large events occur because of economic conditions. In their Marxist view of History, one thing is rather striking: most revolutions around the World (French Revolution of 1789, European revolutions of 1848…) were preceded by rapidly rising food prices. And fair enough: when food prices rise rapidly, and the working class can no longer afford to feed itself, it is not a stretch to imagine that the working class gets angry (we have a sister like that;

extremely kind and charming, until she is made to skip a meal, at which point hell hath no fury like...).

Reason #2: Tian An Men 1989. One of the main reasons the leadership massively over-reacted and sent in the tanks to break the student demonstrations was that, in the early days of June, the students had started to gain the support of Beijing's factory workers. What had until then remained a demonstration of thousands of students around the country risked degenerating into a full-scale demonstration against the regime. And what were the workers demonstrating against? Rapidly rising inflation, and especially food prices. This is why the generation of leaders which came in the wake of Tian An Men (Jiang Zemin, Zhu Rongji...) were such inflation hawks.

This perspective helps explain why each time food price inflation rears its ugly head (basically, each time there is a very bad harvest), the Chinese government is forced to introduce restrictive measures to cool down the economy (and prices). As we wrote in July 2004 in one of our Five Corners reports:

"One of the financial markets' big surprises this year has been the degree to which the Chinese leadership has seemed hell-bent on slowing down China's impressive growth. Measures have included raises in the bank's reserve requirements, tightening of lending to specific sectors (steel, autos, construction...) and pressures on local authorities to trim their spending.

But why would China's leadership aim to curb growth given the country's continued needs for infrastructure spending (roads, power plants, schools, hospital)? Why is growth a problem when policy makers still fret about the army of unemployed workers for whom jobs need to be found? How else but through growth will the loss-making SOEs be reformed? For the Chinese leadership, growth became a problem at the beginning of that year for one main reason: the fact that inflation in China had once again been rearing its ugly head. China's urban migration requires massive capital spending: housing, schools, sewer systems, power plants, transport system... all need to be built if China is to avoid its cities spurring shanty-towns such as Cairo, Lagos, Calcutta etc...

As we have highlighted in many reports over the past year, most of the inflation has come from food prices (up +12% YoY). And given that food spending accounts for 40% of the median Chinese family's income, rapid food price inflation is today a problem which could conceivably trigger a crisis (after all, every single revolution has found its source in rapid food price inflation).

Interestingly, the food price inflation is not taking place where one would expect it (big and booming cities), but in the poor countryside. *And when we think about it, this makes sense.*

Indeed, over the past few years, China has had both food crisis (i.e.: bird flu) and bad harvests (after a remarkable expansion of grain output from 90 million tons in 1950 to 392 million tons in 1998, China's grain harvest has fallen in four of the last five years - dropping to 322 million tons in 2003. For perspective, this drop of 70 million tons exceeds the entire grain harvest of Canada).

And this is where China's transport infrastructure problems come into the limelight again: ***while it is easy for China to buy grain abroad and distribute it in the main cities, distributing the grain in the countryside is far more challenging.*** *Hence the higher countryside food price inflation…."*

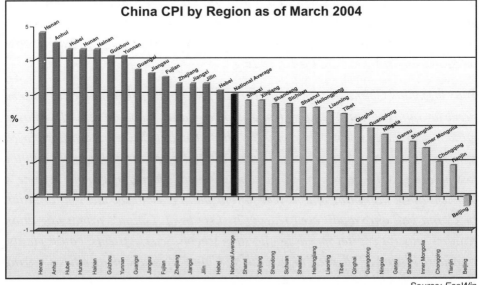

Source: EcoWin

This leaves us with the belief that we can probably trust the Chinese leadership when they tell us that they are on hold until at least October. Indeed, the Chinese leadership is now waiting for the September harvest. If the harvest is good, the leadership will let the economy roar. If the harvest is bad, it will need to take control of China's transport system to move grain, and nothing else, around."

As it turned out, the September 2004 harvest was a strong one, so the economy was allowed to go on a tear once again.

But this still leaves China today in the current odd situation where, when the harvests are weak, food price inflation is higher in the countryside than in the cities for the simple reason that, when harvests are weak, China can simply use up some of its massive reserves and import rice, grains, chicken or beef. These foodstuffs can then be delivered cheaply and efficiently into the cities… but not in the countryside. The logistical systems simply do not exist today to allow the foodstuffs to move around.

However, as the logistical systems to move goods around more efficiently are being put into place today, we can probably look to the future with more enthusiasm. For example, the road construction program mentioned above should ensure that, in the event of poor harvests, food will reach the countryside in a timely and cost-efficient manner. And, in turn, this will hopefully allow the government to not have to panic and slam on the brakes at the first whiff of a bad harvest.

The fact that infrastructure is being put in place to deliver goods and services ever further afield should also end up having important microeconomic consequences. Indeed, taking the US interstate as an example, and as mentioned above, the interstate system allowed a company like Wal-Mart to thrive and rapidly cover an area the size of a continent. So who will be the companies able to best leverage the new infrastructure and turn it into profits for their shareholders the way Wal-Mart did it in the US, Tesco in the UK, or Carrefour in France?

Maybe it will simply be Carrefour or Wal-Mart? Or maybe it will be a domestic company like Lianhua Supermarkets? A few years ago, before the deregulation mentioned in the previous chapter, the safer bet would have been Lianhua. After all, Lianhua is China's largest food retailer in terms of number of stores (its stores are concentrated in Shanghai and nearby towns). But today, the picture is no longer clear-cut:

Competition in Lianhua's core Shanghai market is becoming very fierce as the total number of hypermarkets has tripled from 40-50 in 2001 to more than 150 today. Worse yet, competition in the second and third tier cities is becoming keener, as foreign operators can more easily move into these areas. Consequently, the company's sales in 2005 only rose 17%, a much lower pace than the +59% in sales registered in 2003, or the +29% registered in 2001 and 2002....

At this stage, finding out which company will benefit the most from China's impressive infrastructure spending, industry deregulation, growing means of communications and rapidly rising education levels would be no more than guess-work. **But we can be confident of one thing: the Chinese consumer will be a major beneficiary of the trends highlighted above.**

The Acceleration Phenomenon

In the previous chapters, we have reviewed how:

- Chinese incomes are rising thanks to productivity gains (which find their source either in workers leaving unproductive agriculture behind, young people achieving higher education levels, etc…)

- prices are falling thanks to deregulation, privatization, infrastructure spending, etc…

So people have more money and an ever-increasing number of goods keep falling in price? Should we be surprised that China is undergoing an unprecedented consumer spending boom?

In _Our Brave New World,_ we discussed at length the concept of acceleration. This concept was first developed by Aftalion, a French economist, at the beginning of the XXth century. Aftalion explained that most socio-economic variables are distributed according to the **"normal law"**, the famous bell-shaped curve, affectionately also called the boiler hat. In other words, income is distributed according to a Gaussian pattern, with a large percentage of the population having an income close to the 'average' income. There will be few people with a very low income and few with a very high income. At both ends of the curve (the tails), one finds a very small population in percentage terms.

Assume that, in a given country, the average income in 1985 was US$5,000/year. The number of people earning more than US$10,000 would be, for example, 5%. If, by 1990, this average income goes up to US$8,000 (+60%), the number of people earning more than US$10,000 would not rise by 60%, but by a much larger figure (say 180%).

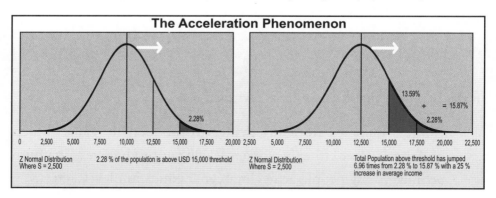

The Acceleration Phenomenon

And this is where the acceleration comes in: when it comes to the buying of certain goods and services, the historical evidence seems to suggest the existence of "thresholds". For example, if the average income in a country is below US$1,000, nobody owns a television; when the income moves above US$1,000, then almost everybody buys one. For the automobile industry, the critical level seems to be US$10,000/year, for tourism US$15,000, for university education US$20,000, for private savings products (i.e.: life insurance, mutual funds …) US$30,000....

So, in the country chosen as an example, when the average income reaches US$10,000, the demand for cars will literally explode way beyond the correspondent growth in income. Acceleration works in a very surprising way. Similarly, if the average income falls from US$10,000 to US$8,000, the demand for cars will not decline by -20%, but will disappear (this is what we witnessed in Indonesia in the 1997-1998 Asian crisis; new car sales literally ground to a halt).

At the same time, if the price of a good falls, then the threshold level falls with it. A quick example: in 1999, there were practically no mobile phone subscribers in China. But as incomes rose and the price of phone calls and handsets fell, the market for mobile phones in China evolved from being nonexistent to becoming the world's largest (around 400 million people now have mobiles in China).

As incomes rise in China, various thresholds are crossed (first TV, then mobile phones, then autos, then tourism...) and consumption explodes. The boom in consumption is boosted further by the fall in certain prices (electronics, automobiles, etc...). This acceleration phenomenon is what makes deflationary booms possible.

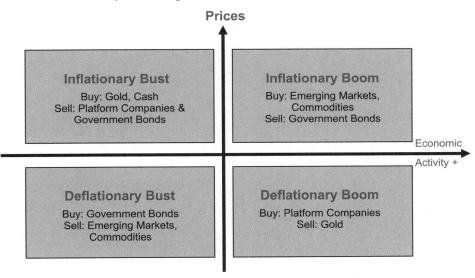

In recent years China has gone through a massive deflationary boom. Prices of manufactured goods fell (though food and energy prices are on the rise), and consumption boomed. In fact, in the 3Q06, for the first time since 2001, consumption growth (as measured by retail sales), exceeded nominal GDP growth (13.5% vs 13.3%). This is a healthy development which underlines that Chinese growth can continue at a high rate even if the rate of investment and trade growth slows somewhat in the next year or two.

China's Demographic Sweet-Spot

There is no more self-evident truth than the hackneyed-saying that "demographics is destiny". The babies who are not born today are unlikely to become workers in twenty years time. So with that in mind, a review of China's demographic structure is always going to be important. And today, the Chinese demographic reality is the topic of much debate.

As things stand, most people agree that China is currently in a demographic "sweet spot". The changes in the pyramid of ages shown on the following pages show the typical demographic picture of a society getting richer with the usual main characteristics of a) people growing older as healthcare and diets improve, b) less children as people move from the farm into the cities and c) an ever-improving "dependency-ratio" whereby most people are aged between 15 and 55 years old and are thus working, saving, and consuming and (unlike young children or older folks) not draining society's resources.

In 1990, China offered the typical "third world" pyramid of ages, namely a society full of young children, and scarce in old people (people died young).

Now witness, by 2006, the transformation. All of a sudden, there are a lot less young kids, and a lot more adults. Best of all, as far as "societal costs" are concerned, there are no "old people" yet. In 2006, in China, a majority of people are working, saving and consuming (incidentally, immigration countries such as the US or Australia offer this kind of pyramid of ages year in, year out thanks to the fact that these countries attract 20- to 40-year olds to their shores).

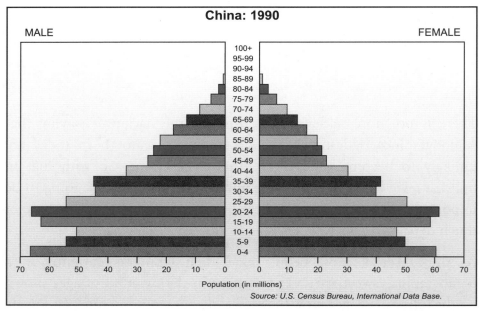

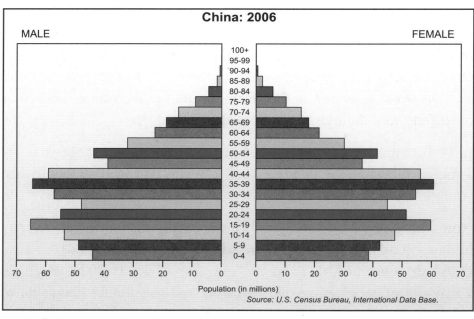

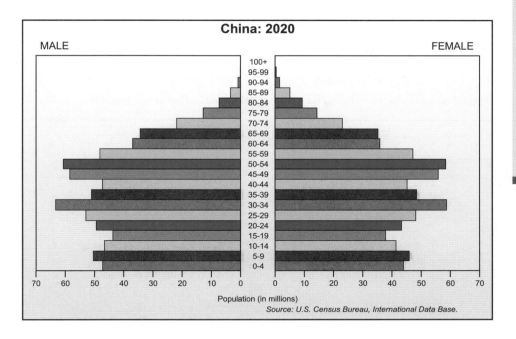

China: 2020

MALE

FEMALE

Population (in millions)

Source: U.S. Census Bureau, International Data Base.

This demographic structure whereby the majority of the population are young adults is, of course, great news for Chinese real estate. If nothing else, it guarantees a constant demand for housing.

But of course, the above charts raise the question of how long China will remain in the "demographic sweet-spot". Following official data, one would be tempted to conclude that China will remain in the sweet-spot for at least another decade.

However, this assertion, and the data on which it is built, is currently the source of much debate. A number of scholars, Dr Clint Laurent of *Asia Demographics* chief amongst them, have lately been highlighting some interesting contradictions.

Following the 2000 census, it was assumed that Chinese births were a little over 19 million per year, and that this rate would slowly decline to reach 17 million by 2003. With these numbers, one could assume that the Chinese working population would grow steadily and then start declining (mildly) in 2014. However, some recent numbers have come to shed some doubt on this optimistic scenario and the Chinese population, and the Chinese workforce could start peaking as early as 2008.

The first part of the explanation is that China, in recent years, had probably registered far more births than the country has in fact experienced. Why?

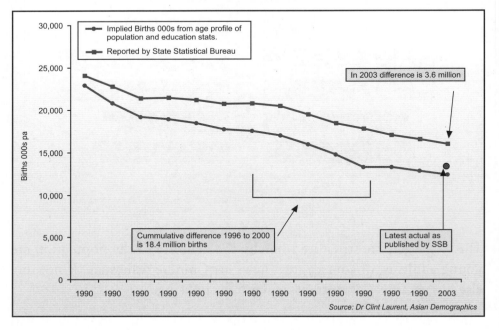

Source: Dr Clint Laurent, Asian Demographics

Most likely because hospitals, in order to maintain their level of funding, might have registered more births than took place. One explanation is that some Chinese hospitals may have counted some abortions as births in order to get extra money from the central government.

The State Statistical Bureau nearly admitted as such when it recently massively downgraded its number for 2003 births by 3.6 million. Now how did the SSB know something was wrong with the data? Simple enough: the data of Chinese number of births simply did not match the data for school enrolments. Year in and year out, over 3 million children would go "missing", thereby leading to the following potential conclusions:

- The 3 million missing kids were held back by parents from going to school–a very unlikely possibility in a culture which highly values education.

- The 3 million kids had died in the four years before going to school–a very unlikely possibility given the improvements in medicine, eating habits etc... prevalent today in China.

- The 3 million kids were never born in the first place and hospitals made them up to get extra funding.

With the little we know about China, and its officials' healthy disregard for budgets, we would pick the third option. Apparently, so has the SSB.

This revision in the birth rates has a number of important consequences. The first, and most evident one, is that China's workforce could grow less fast than currently expected by the market. As Dr. Clint Laurent highlights in the following charts, the Chinese economy took on an additional 77 million workers between 1994 and 2004. And most people today believe that this rate of growth in the number of workers will continue unabated. But the near future might show this to be a false hope. In the period 2004-2009, China could add as little as an additional 20 million net new jobs (i.e.: half the previous pace) and starting in 2009, China could actually start to lose workers.

If Dr. Laurent's data is to be trusted, the second very important demographic development is that China's population starts ageing much earlier than previously anticipated. In fact, and again according to Dr Laurent, by 2024, the single biggest age group in the Chinese population should be the 40-59 range; a marked departure from previous belief which held that the 25-39 age group would remain the most important for decades to come.

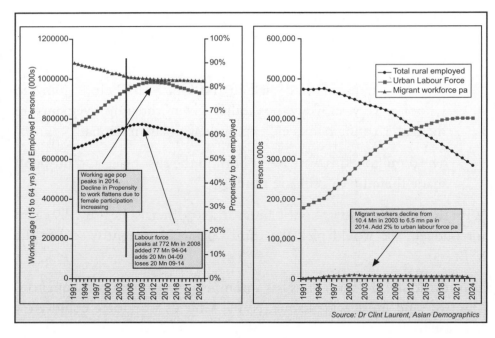

Source: Dr Clint Laurent, Asian Demographics

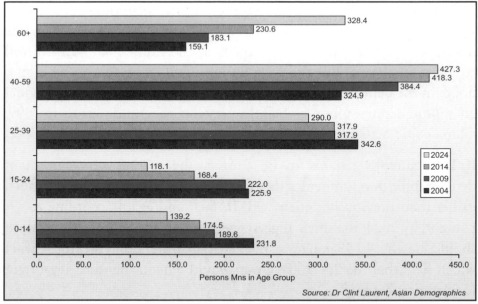

Source: Dr Clint Laurent, Asian Demographics

Now why does this matter? Because the demographic change could end up having a big impact on Chinese consumption patterns. In most nations, including China, income is distributed according to a Gaussian pattern, a large percentage of the population having an income close to the "average" income. There will be few people with a very low income and few with a very high income. At both ends of the curve (the tails), one finds a very small population in percentage terms.

Why is this important? Because, as we highlighted in a previous chapter, when it comes to the buying of certain goods and services, the historical evidence seems to suggest the existence of "thresholds". For example, if the average income in a country is below US$1,000, nobody owns a television; when the income moves above US$1,000, then almost everybody buys one. For the automobile industry, the critical level seems to be US$10,000/year. For university education US$20,000, For financial products US$30,000 …

But having said, different demographics present different threshold points; 59-year olds and 25-year olds do not consume the same things. So China's rapidly changing demographics could prove a boon to companies that sell "experiences" (tourism, entertainment, luxury goods…) and a drag to companies that sell "things" (cars? appliances? video games?). This is an important development possibly not priced into financial markets today.

The change in China's demographic structure is so important that the question needs to be asked of whether it can be reversed? Could Chinese people start having more babies? After all, the big drop in birth rates partly found its source in the "one-child" policy, a policy which is now being loosened, especially for those wealthy enough to provide for several children. And, as we know, the ranks of the wealthy are growing…

China, because of the one-child policy, is indeed in a very odd and historically unprecedented situation. Usually, poor countries register very high birth rates, and, as they get richer, the birth rates drop off. However, in China, the drop-off in the birth rate was organized by political, not economic, forces. And given that the one-child policy is now being loosened, one might hope for a birth revival. But then again, one's hopes might quickly be crushed.

Indeed, despite the relaxing of the one child policy, birth rates have continued to drop and the trend is still heading lower. Moreover, with an accelerating rate of urban migration, it would be surprising to see a surge in births. People in the countryside tend to have more children, for they are less constrained by space. In the cities, however (and especially in Chinese cities!), space is tighter, and children are fewer.

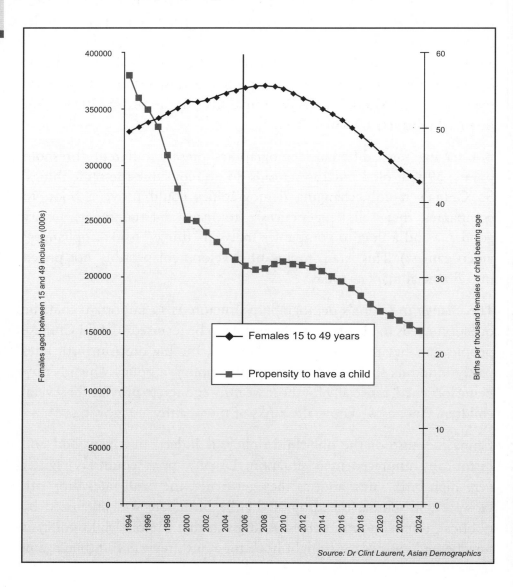

Source: Dr Clint Laurent, Asian Demographics

But the most important factor which should constrain China's demographic growth in the coming decades is that, from our experience, it is necessary to have women around to give birth to babies. And, unfortunately, in China today, the number of women of child bearing age is falling rapidly (partly because a large number of female fetuses were aborted as a direct consequence of the one-child policy).

So given the sharp drop in women of child-bearing age, it seems unlikely that China will be able to reverse the demographic trends. This means that, for the next few years, China will continue to enjoy a demographic sweet spot whereby most people are working, saving and consuming. However, in twenty years' time, the largest demographic segment in China will be the 40-59 year olds. This fact could end up having a deep impact on consumption. Around that time, China will be starting to get old, which of course raises the question of how China will cope with being the first country in History to get old before it got rich. But then again, by that point, maybe China will be rich?

CHAPTER 11

Why Do the Chinese Save So Much? And What Will They Do With Their Savings?

According to government statistics, each person in China holds RMB10,787 worth of savings. More interestingly, the growth in Chinese per capita spending has, in the recent economic boom years, outpaced GDP growth. So the Chinese are saving ever more. Indeed, China's savings rate appears to have been well over 40% of GDP for most of the past decade. This begs the question of "why do the Chinese save so much?"

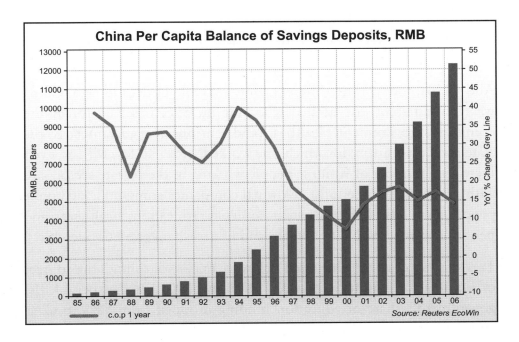

The first simple answer is because half of them work on the farm. As we never tire of writing, there is no worse business than farming: one never knows what tomorrow will be made of. Given the inability to forecast the next harvest, or the coming weather, farmers everywhere have always needed to save a significant portion of their disposable incomes.

The second, just as simple, answer is that the Chinese save because they are poor, and because they have a lot to worry about. Or, to sound smarter: because the transition from planned to market economy has involved a massive shift of financial risk from state-owned enterprises to households, thereby creating a large perceived need for precautionary saving by households to fund anticipated retirement, medical and educational expenses.

The reason people anywhere save is:

a) to create a cushion in the case of a rainy day,

b) build a nest-egg for one's old age, and

c) provide one's children with the same, or better, opportunities than those one enjoyed.

And China, today, is no different. But, a couple of decades ago, China was very different: the limited schooling on offer was paid for by the communist government. Healthcare and pensions were guaranteed by the state-owned company for which one worked, etc... Today, with an ever-increasing number of Chinese people working in the private sector, and with a growing number of state-owned companies going under, Chinese people have found that, when it comes to education, healthcare and pensions, it is advisable to save up and not trust anyone but oneself.

This shifting of risk is illustrated below in a table that shows the sources of funding for education between 1993 and 2003. In that period, the government's share of education funding dropped from 82% to 62%, and the household share rose by a corresponding amount.

Chapter II

Sources of educational funds, 1993-2003
(All levels of education, % of total)

	1993	1998	1999	2000	2001	2002	2003
Government funds	82	69	68	67	66	64	62
Tuition	8	13	14	15	16	17	18
Other	10	18	18	18	18	19	20

Source: National Bureau of Statistics Dragonomics.

At this stage, it is important to acknowledge that less than half of the household contribution to educational expenditure takes the form of tuition (the level of which is regulated by the state). The rest comes through various ad hoc (and often illegal) fees charged to parents by schools to make up for funding shortfalls. A similar (and in some ways more dire) situation has arisen with respect to medical care, with hospitals frequently demanding cash payment in advance for many treatments.

It appears that, in China, precautionary saving for future costs considerably outstrip spending on current costs. This makes sense given that:

• The actual level of future costs and future revenues is, for most Chinese, highly unpredictable.

• The services that people tend to save for (education, healthcare…) are showing much higher price inflation than other goods and services (the health, education and housing components of the consumer price index have been rising at rates of 5-8%, while prices of most other goods and services are static or falling).

The third, more complicated answer to the question of "Why do the Chinese save so much?" goes as such: it is important to remember that household saving is only one component of national saving. Corporate and government savings can also have an impact on the national savings rate. And, as it turns out, these latter sources of savings do much to explain why China's saving rate is so much higher than other countries.

On the Corporate Saving Side: Corporate savings have been high recently because of greatly increased corporate profitability in the 2000-2006 period. Profits have been rising not only in the fast-growing private sector, but also in the state sector (which was substantially restructured following 1998 and forced many loss-making state enterprises to exit the market). Now rising corporate profitability translates less quickly into consumption in China than in other countries, because **most companies are not publicly listed, and most pay little or nothing in dividends.**

In the US or in Europe, when corporate profits rise, stock prices and dividends also tend to rise. Shareholders can easily sell or borrow against their stock holdings to finance consumption, and they may also choose to spend, rather than re-invest, some of their dividend income. In China these transmission mechanisms do not exist, so profits tend to stay within the companies that generated them (and get disproportionately funneled into new investment).

Structure of savings in China and other countries % of GDP:

	China	US	France	Japan	Korea	Mexico
Total domestic savings	45.0	14.3	20.7	25.5	31.0	20.8
Difference China/others		30.7	24.3	19.5	14.0	24.2
Due to:						
Household saving		13.4	7.4	10.0	13.7	10.2
Corporate saving		9.6	10.4	0.5	5.1	9.3
Government saving		7.8	6.6	9.1	-4.8	4.7

Note: data for China is for 2004, for Mexico for 2001, and for other countries for 2002.

Source: Louis Kuijs (World Bank); figures derived from OECD and China National Bureau of Statistics

On the Government Spending Side: Government saving represents the difference between government revenue and government consumption expenditure. Now talking of government spending in China may seem nonsensical given that China's government runs a persistent budget deficit of 1-3% of GDP. But despite apparent budget deficits, China's fiscal policy has been conservative (at least by developing-country standards). Indeed, about 60% of government expenditure goes into consumption (health, military, education, administration...), while 40% is invested in infrastructure. This is a very healthy proportion of spending skewed towards infrastructure.

On the positive side, this policy avoids the common Third World trap of running up large debts to finance unproductive expenditure. It is also positive for economic growth, since investment in roads, communication networks and power plants produce long-term returns and help boost productivity.

On the negative side, and as noted above, this policy shifts the burden of financing social welfare to households, and compels them to maintain a high rate of savings. **Low government consumption thus leads directly to low household consumption.**

And finally, there is a fourth, and completely untested, explanation (or, more like, theory) to the recent pick-up in the Chinese savings rate: demographic trends. To illustrate this theory, let us ask our reader a few questions:

- Who, in the Western world, has the worst savings rate? The US.

- Who has the highest savings' rate? Japan, Italy and Germany...

- Who has the best demographic trends? The US.

- Who has the worst demographic trends? Japan, Italy, Germany...

Putting these questions and answers together, should we not conclude that there is a direct link between demography and savings? Is the fact that the highest savers in the world also have the worst demographics a pure coincidence? And, as regards to China, should we be surprised that, as China nears its population peak (more on that later), its savings rate accelerates?

After all kids cost money, a lot of it, and everyday a little more (look at how education costs have steadily risen faster than inflation for the past two decades). So if nothing else, we should expect people that do not have kids to save more than people who do.

But even beyond that, remember that kids, in most poorer nations, have historically always been a guarantee for one's old age. Victor Hugo's adage that "a father can feed eight kids, but eight kids cannot feed one father" has definitely never been a part of Chinese culture! In Chinese culture, the young are supposed to take care of the old. Though, after two generations of "one-child policy", this old pattern has definitely been turned on its head.

Jean Bodin famously said, "There is no wealth but Man". If your average Chinese man and woman are now forced, by law, to produce less children, should we be surprised by the reflex of storing up wealth in other forms?

And this is where it gets cruelly unjust. Imagine that you are a Chinese citizen in advanced middle age. Twenty-five years ago, you were told that you could only have one child. You then lost your job (along with your pension and healthcare) at the state owned-company at which you worked (a little known fact, but in the 1997-98 economic downturn, Chinese industry fired more workers than there are industrial workers in America). You found another job and increased your spending to reflect the fact that:

- No one would take care of you in your old age

- Healthcare costs keep rising faster than your wages

- Your job security has all but disappeared

As the table on the following page suggests, only a minority of Chinese citizens are covered by any kind of pension scheme. And given the above, an increase in saving is a perfectly rational decision.

Pension coverage, 1990-2005

Contributors + recipients as % of:					
	Contributors mn	Recipients mn	Total population	Urban population	Urban workers
1990	52	10	5.4	20.4	30.5
1995	87	22	9.1	31.2	45.9
2000	105	32	10.7	29.7	45.1
2005	131	44	13.4	31.1	48.0

Source: Whiteford and Adema, using NBS data.

This is all the more true when one considers that very few people have any kind of medical coverage and that individuals by and large still have to foot the bill of any medical procedures:

Structure of China's health care financing 1996-2005

	Total expenditure Rmb bn	Share of Total		
		Social insurance, %	Government outlays, %	Individuals, %
1996	271	29	18	53
1997	320	27	17	56
1998	368	23	19	58
1999	405	22	19	59
2000	459	22	16	62
2001	503	20	16	64
2002	579	20	16	64
2003	658	19	17	64
2004	759	21	17	62
2005	866	21	18	61

Source: Ministry of Health.

And that, these bills can represent a large percentage of the average citizen's disposable income:

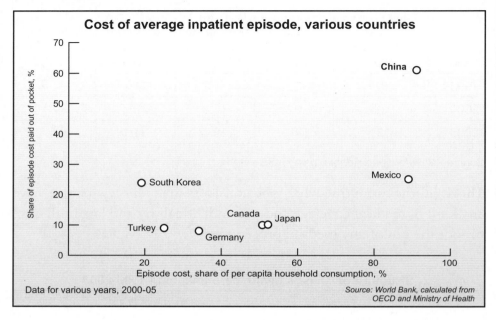

Cost of average inpatient episode, various countries

Data for various years, 2000-05

Source: World Bank, calculated from OECD and Ministry of Health

Looking at the above data, one may be tempted to a) feel glad not to be the "average Chinese citizen" and b) despair at the possibility of ever seeing a consumer led economy emerge in China.

But this would be taking a "glass half empty" view of things. Indeed, on the positive side one may hope that, as China's insurance industry matures, and as the Chinese government cranks up its social spending in a bid to create a "harmonious society", we could conceivably see the very high Chinese saving rate fall, and consumption rise.

The Costs of China's Impressive Growth: An Environmental Challenge

For those of us caught in the middle of it, there is little doubt that China is attempting to achieve, over twenty years, levels of economic expansion that most countries took a century to achieve. China is raising a majority of its population out of poverty, building first-world level infrastructure, reshaping a financial system, reconstructing its cities… and all this in a very short period of time. There is also little doubt that this accelerated pace of growth comes at a price. And, so far, it often feels as if Mother Nature has been paying the bills.

We could ramble for pages on the environmental devastation taking place in China. After all, it is now the single biggest topic of conversation amongst expats in Hong Kong (who arguably have little else to complain about, save the crazy real estate prices). Still, the pollution coming down the Pearl River Delta is now so thick that, on many days, we cannot even see the other side of Victoria Harbor from our Central Plaza office, let alone the beautiful peaks of the New Territories.

But beyond the very visible "bad-air" problem, China's main environmental challenge, and growth constraint, is actually water. Indeed, China faces a double water problem: much of it is unfit to drink, and there is not enough of it to go around.

In a paper that we published back in 2005, our colleague Tom Miller wrote: "China's annual per capita water availability stands at around 2,200 tons, just 25 percent of the global average, but still above the United

Nations-defined 1,750-tonne "threshold of concern". The government reckons that water shortage will become most acute in 2030, when a population of 1.6bn will have just 1,760 tons of water per person. At the same time–no surprise here–China is among the world's least efficient users of water, consuming around 400kg of water to produce a dollar of GDP, more than ten times the American ratio.

These figures are bad enough, yet they hide something worse: the divide between China's water-rich south and the north, where water levels are perilously low. In the north China plain, which sweeps from Beijing in the north to Jiangsu province in the south, average water resources per head are around 500 tons, or half the UN's "danger" threshold of 1,000 tons. Tianjin, the driest city in the region, has a per capita water resource less than that of Saudi Arabia. Out of China's 660 cities, more than 400 lack sufficient water supplies, and 110 suffer from serious shortages.

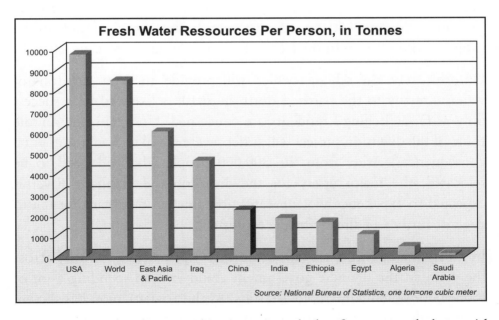

Looking into the future, China's serious lack of water, and the rapid desertification of some regions (Ningxia, Inner Mongolia, Gansu…) should lead to three events:

1. Large engineering projects to bring water to water-poor counties:
Whenever confronted with a resource problem, the Chinese government's
usual inclination is to "throw money, and labor, at the problem" and see
what happens. As far as the water issue is concerned, this means devising
massive infrastructure projects to bring water from water-rich regions to
thirsty regions.

The keystone of national water management engineering is the 50-year,
US$60bn South-North water diversion project, which will divert millions
of tons of Yangtze River water to the north China plain. The scheme is
divided into three routes: a short "western route" diverting water from the
upper Yangtze tributaries within the Sichuan and Qinghai mountains; a
"middle route" diverting water from the Danjiankou reservoir on the
Hanjiang River, a major tributary of the middle Yangtze, to Beijing; and
the "eastern route", which will take water from the lower reaches of the
Yangtze, 100km south of Nanjing, to Tianjin. The entire scheme is set
for completion by 2050, but the first water from the middle route of the
project should flow into the lake at Beijing's Summer Palace in 2010.

Unfortunately, the scheme, which will provide an extra 1bn tons of
water annually to the parched north in 2010, is likely to be a success
only as far as Beijing's residents are concerned. Upstream, the middle
route of the diversion project will suffer severe social and environmental
consequences. Aside from the 300,000 people who will need to be
relocated, the major artery for the diversion–the Hanjiang River–is
expected to experience violent water flow fluctuations that threaten to
degrade further an already fragile ecosystem.

In short, in an effort to spread the limited "water wealth" equally across
the country, the Chinese government could end up spending a lot of
money, for potentially dubious results. As the Soviet Union has shown,
toying with ecosystems can lead to profound and lasting disasters.

2. A needed reform of agriculture: Agriculture matters far more than
industrial or residential water use, for two reasons. First, agriculture
consumes 65% of China's water, compared to 25% for industry and 10%

for residential users. Second, agricultural water can only be used once, since crops absorb the water and then respire it out. Substantial fractions of industrial and residential water, by contrast, can be recycled for repeat use. Reducing water use in agriculture is thus the crucial challenge of China's leadership.

And there is, of course an easy way to do this: raising the price of water. Indeed, despite modest increases since 1985 (when water was still free) China's average water price remains ridiculously low–about 16 US cents (Rmb2) per cubic meter, compared to US$2.50 per cubic meter in America. As such, China's water price is completely unrelated either to water's scarcity or to the actual cost of delivery. So can the Chinese government remove the water subsidy? We tend to believe that, given the environmental destruction, the Politburo cannot avoid removing the subsidy in the coming years.

Of course, the removal of water subsidies is a hornet's nest as far as the Chinese government is concerned. The government realizes that, because of environmental imperatives, it does not really have an alternative; but at the same time, removing the water subsidies could create massive rural unrest. Indeed, most Chinese farmers already feel 'left behind" in the country's impressive growth surge. If the government now turns around and tells them: "we realize that you feel left behind, and we are very sorry. By the way, here is your new high water bill", a lot of farmers may not react kindly. And open rebellion in the countryside is the last thing the Communist Party, which claims to have its roots amongst China's peasants, wants to see.

Yet, there is little doubt that as the water subsidies are removed, a lot of farms in China will become economically unviable. They will thus release millions of workers into the cities.

Over the past decade, China's cities have added approximately 100 million people. Such a rapid urbanisation represents one of the most dramatic population shifts in History. And so far, it has presented China with both challenges and opportunities. In fact, around 80% of China's growth in the past ten years has come from its cities. At the same time, China has added nearly 200 "new" cities. The Asian Development Bank estimates that the number of people in urban areas will expand from 360 million today to 700 million by 2010.

So far, China, through impressive infrastructure spending projects, and by limiting the scope of internal migration (Hukou system), has managed to avoid the emergence of "tin-cities" such as Lagos, Rio, or Mexico City.... Nevertheless, if following a removal of the water subsidy, the pace of internal migration picks up, will China be able to accommodate all of the new urbanites? Where will those ex-farmhands work? Where will they live?

The deregulation of the housing/registration policy is unleashing a new wave of growth around China. But it also presents huge challenges to which the government is responding by accelerating deregulation (i.e.: home ownership schemes, mortgage industry growth, deregulation of the utilities industries, relaxation of foreign ownership rules on logistic and transport companies...).

The urban migration currently happening across China and Asia requires massive capital spending. Housing, schools, sewer systems, power plants, transport systems... all need to be built. Governments have little choice but to gun for growth. Indeed, the Chinese government is not letting itself be taken by surprise. The very real possibility of an important rural exodus explains partly the impressive boom in infrastructure spending (a theme to which I will return later in the book) in China's major, and minor, cities.

CHAPTER **13**

Isn't China at Risk of Social Upheaval?

In our meetings with clients around the world, we are frequently asked how long it will be before the internal contradictions in China's development model will start tearing the country apart. Even beyond the environmental constraints, we are told that China's current political arrangement can not last. And is this not a major risk to any world view which sees the economic growth of China as a sturdy rock? "Perhaps", is always our (polite) answer to such questions. But then again, one can maybe look at China as dealing with the problems it has been confronting in an ever-more efficient manner. My colleague Arthur Kroeber does just that in the following pages:

Chinese History since the start of rule by the Chinese Communist Party in 1949 can be divided into three phases, each roughly spanning a generation. The first, from 1949 through 1978, was the socialist era during which Mao Zedong's government attempted to impose a centrally planned economy. This effort brought a number of disastrous consequences, notably the failed industrialization of the Great Leap Forward (1956-59) which led to the famine of 1960-62 in which 30-40m people died; and the increasing reliance on rule by terror which shattered an entire generation of intellectuals and technocrats, and led to virtual civil war during the Cultural Revolution (1966-69).

But this era also generated some real achievements, which laid the groundwork for the growth of later decades. The first was political unification. Until 1912 China was ruled by a medieval imperial autocracy which presided over a large, complex but essentially Malthusian economy in which technological gains were immediately offset by a rise in population with the result that per-capita incomes scarcely ever rose. After the fall of the traditional state there ensued four decades of political entropy during which no effective central authority emerged and there were few if any widespread social and economic gains. The CCP, with extreme brutality, created the stable framework of a modern state, which is a major prerequisite of economic modernization. Decades later, the state framework established in the 1950s persists and grows stronger, even though virtually all vestiges of the Communist ideology used to create it have vanished.

Because of its effectiveness at mass mobilization, the CCP also engineered major improvements in health care and education. Average life expectancy rose from 45 years in 1950 to nearly 70 years in 1980, thanks to improved hygiene, vaccinations and control of epidemic disease. Literacy rose from under 10% to around 90% in the same period. These gains generated substantial legitimacy for the regime, and helped offset its incompetence and terrorism in other areas. They were indispensable in creating a work-force capable of entering the global economy. The socialist era also produced two economic policies with lasting consequences:

1. One was land collectivization, accomplished with great savagery during the 1950s. The immediate consequence was baleful: the elimination of individual farmer incentives was a major cause of the great famine. And even after that, in the later 1960s and 1970s, agricultural productivity rose more slowly than would have been the case in a freer system. But collectivization did destroy the old concentrations of land ownership, and after individual incentives were restored in the early 1980s the egalitarian land-holding structure provided a firm foundation for rapid economic growth, as was previously the case in Japan, South Korea and Taiwan. Egalitarian land holding prevents agricultural surpluses from being hoarded as rents by a narrow landed elite; instead they can be captured by the state and funneled into industrialization.

2. The second was a surprising level of industrial decentralization–surprising because China ostensibly followed the Soviet Union planned economy model. Although on the surface China had the same centralized configuration of state planning commission and industrial ministries as the Soviet Union, in reality economic decision-making was far more dispersed. Thanks to Mao's predilection for local autarky, every province and major city had a more or less complete set of light industrial plants producing the necessities of urban life. Even heavy industrial production was duplicated in several locations because of the national security concern that highly concentrated industrial centers would leave China vulnerable to damaging air strikes in the event of war. The consequence was that when local officials were given economic growth incentives in the 1980s, most had plenty of tools to work with.

The second era in CCP rule took off in late 1978 with the Party Congress that brought Deng Xiaoping to power, although the groundwork had been laid in 1973 when Deng was called back from political exile to rebuild an economy staggering from excesses of ideologically-driven policy during the Cultural Revolution. Deng inherited an economy that, despite its improved basic infrastructure, did a poor job of raising per capita incomes. His pragmatic goal was simply to make the economy work better. His serendipitous stroke of political genius was to coin a slogan for his reform program that has proved indestructible through 30 years of dramatic economic and social upheaval: *gaige kaifang*, or "reform and opening."

Unlike Japan, South Korea and Taiwan, which developed behind high tariff walls and with little foreign investment, China recognized that its domestic economic reform program (*gaige*) was inextricably linked to escalating engagement with the global economy (*kaifang*), through both exports and inbound direct investment. Yet the goal of Chinese economic reform, despite persistent misunderstanding by foreign observers, was never to create a Western-style capitalist economy. There was in fact no model, or pre-determined end point for the reform process. There were, however, three underlying principles from which the country's leadership has not deviated to this day:

1. The economy must be made progressively more effective at generating wealth.

2. The state must retain a substantial direct ownership role in the economy.

3. The CCP must retain absolute control of the political system.

Westerners immediately grasped principle number 1, and frequently–through a combination of false analogies and mistaking effect for cause–reasoned that because all advanced economies were political democracies with limited state ownership of economic assets, that principles 2 and 3 inevitably conflicted with principle 1 and would therefore have to be abandoned. Over and over and over again for the past thirty years, foreign analysts have lectured China about how its "partial" or "piecemeal" moves to a market capitalist economy left it in an "unsustainable half-way house" and that abandonment of the principle of state ownership was the only way to sustain progress. Time and again foreigners have declared that the combination of a dynamic economy with a static political system was intrinsically unstable, and that popular pressure from the "rising middle class", the "disgruntled rural masses", or "dynamic entrepreneurs" would necessitate dramatic political reforms–failing which economic growth would grind slower or even halt against the resistance of these political contradictions.

Sub specie aeternitatis, these arguments are probably more true than false. And it is most unlikely that China will enter the 22nd century–or even the second half of the 21st–without either a reasonably representative system of government or a far higher proportion of the economy in private hands. For the time being, however, Deng's reform program has delivered a remarkably stable synthesis in which adherence to all three principles has been strengthened. The structural distortions of the centrally planned economy have been mostly eliminated. Prices are determined by the market, except for a handful that most countries manipulate to varying degrees, notably for energy. Most markets, even those dominated by state players, have a significant degree of competition. Since the mid-1990s, China has sustained GDP growth of around 10% a year and inflation of under 5% a year. State control of assets has been streamlined and made more effective; CCP political authority is unchallenged.

The nature of China's economy today is best understood through its ownership structure. The state sector accounts for about 35% of output, and it decisively controls all upstream and network sectors of the economy –as it were, the skeleton and musculature of the nation's economic body. Natural resource extraction, transport, telecommunications, power generation and distribution, oil refining, and the production of key materials such as steel and basic petrochemicals, along with many machinery and national defense related industries, are all in state hands, and moreover the assets in these sectors are progressively being consolidated in the hands of a smaller number of larger companies with ever more professional management.

Much has been made of the dramatic decline in the state's share of the economy over the past 20 years. But much of this decline is more apparent than real. Partly this has to do with misleading statistics. The standard series on industrial production, for instance, can be made to show that state firms now account for just 10% of industrial output. Yet this figure applies only to traditional, noncorporatized state enterprises; when corporatized state enterprises are included the state share of industry rises to as high as 47%.

More important, Beijing has grasped the principle of *leverage*. In the socialist era, it imagined that in order for the state to exercise effective control over the economy, it had to own 100% of the assets. In the 1990s, it discovered the magical fact that it could sell minority shares in most state-owned enterprises to outside investors, thereby bringing in billions of dollars of capital without ceding an iota of control. In recent years government-linked economists have made the point that direct state control of assets could fall to as low as 10% without materially affecting the state's ultimate role in the economy.

The second component of the economy is the domestic private sector, which accounts for a larger share of output–50% or so and rising. It also generates virtually all net employment growth and earns a return on capital of about 5 percentage points higher than the state sector. Yet it is fragmented among literally hundreds of thousands of small companies whose market power is limited and whose political influence is nil. China has failed to produce any analogues to the great private conglomerates so prominent in most other Asian economies: Japan's Mitsubishi and Mitsui, Korea's Hyundai and LG, India's Tata and Reliance, the far-flung empires of southeast Asian tycoons such as Hong Kong's Li Ka-shing and Malaysia's Robert Kuok. This absence of politically powerful private business groups is not accidental; it is a consequence of deliberate policy aimed at minimizing the political role of the private sector, in the service of principles no. 2. and no. 3–ensuring a strong direct state role in the economy and a political monopoly for the CCP.

Western capitalists observe the efficiency gap between the private and state sector and declare that China faces ruin or stagnation if the "inefficient" state sector does not give way to the "efficient" private sector. This ignores that return on capital has been *rising* at about the same rate in the state sector as in the private; and the state share of overall industrial profits has held steady. As long as this holds there is little economic pressure for the state to cede control of key industries to private hands. Moreover, from a developmental standpoint the large state sector plays an important and potentially beneficial role: it prevents economic rents from being captured by a small group of tycoons who use these cash flows to build empires based on asset trading rather than broad based industrial development. This type of crony capitalism wrecked the Philippines and stymied the economies of other southeast Asian nations; somewhat similar dynamics have played out to bad effect in much of Latin America (*For an insightlul dissection of tycoon culture and its baleful impact on the economies of southeast Asia, see the recent book by our colleague Joe Studwell*; Asian Godfathers).

The final element of China's mixed economy is the foreign sector. This accounts for about 15% of business sector output but nearly 60% of exports, and 90% of exports designated "high tech" by the Chinese government. If the state sector is China's bones and muscles, and the private sector the flesh and blood, the foreign sector is like a Power Bar. It is the conduit by which key nutrients–new technology and expertise–are continuously introduced into the Chinese economy, and it is probably the ultimate source of most of the productivity improvement in China beyond the gains achieved by the brute application of large amounts of capital to large amounts of labor.

This very obvious foreign dependence has led many analysts to suggest that slower growth in the rest of the world spells trouble for China (see next chapter for more on this topic). But this view crucially misunderstands the difference between China's *secular* and *cyclical* relationships with the global economy. On a *secular* basis, as Deng Xiaoping clearly understood when he forced *kaifang* to lock arms with *gaige*, China depends profoundly on the existence of a liberal international economic order with free flows of goods and capital, and on the continuous innovations in hard and soft technologies generated by the advanced open economies, principally the US. If this system suddenly froze up and goods, capital and knowledge stopped flowing around the world, China would face very serious difficulty: partly through a loss of excess demand but more importantly because of a loss of access to the wellsprings of its productivity gains.

On a *cyclical* basis, however, so long as the system remains in place China is so huge that it is virtually unaffected by the peaks and troughs of economic activity elsewhere. Moderately prudent fiscal policy can ensure that if excess demand disappears from the external account–as occurred in 1998-99 and looks to occur once more in 2008-09–direct and indirect government spending can pick up the slack. Because productivity continues to rise rapidly, producers have considerable ability to respond to tighter conditions without a debilitating hit to profitability.

And because capital and transaction costs remain low and are in essence discretionary–depending on how tightly the government chooses to enforce regulatory requirements–budget constraints can be softened until the cycle perks up again. This mechanism is one of the numerous "shock absorbers" in the Chinese economy, which as we have frequently argued in the past, enable China to ride out gyrations in cycles of global demand and commodity prices.

So in short, the economic reform program launched by Deng Xiaoping in 1978 and maintained by his successors has been strikingly successful: China has delivered consistent economic growth of around 10% a year for three decades, and if anything the foundations of domestic demand are stronger, and volatility lower, now than at any point in the last 30 years. Beijing has engineered an economy that works far better than the planned economy of the 1970s, but it has also ensured state control of a comprehensive spread of key assets in the economy, and managed to defuse actual and potential sources of political challenge so that CCP political hegemony is less in doubt now than at any time since the 1970s. It is not too much of a stretch to say that the restructuring of the old planned economy is now complete. **The age during which structural economic reform was job one is now over.**

Over the next decade or two, job one will be not economic but political. As many observers have pointed out, China's governance system is not fully up to the task of running a dynamic capitalist economy with increasingly diverse interest groups. The Chinese leadership agrees on the diagnosis but differs on the cure. Where Westerners would prescribe a strong dose of democracy, Beijing believes that more efficient administration and governance will do the trick. **Hence the third era of CCP rule, the era of governance reform.**

Deng's economic program pragmatically focused on the *substance* of a market economy–prices and competition–and refused to get hung up on the issues of *form* that foreigners obsessed about (private ownership of assets). In the same way, governance reform will focus on substance (more responsive and efficient, and less corrupt, administration) rather than the form (democratic elections). The goal of economic reform in China was simply to create an economy that worked better while preserving the roles of the state and the CCP. Similarly, the goal of governance reform is to create a governance system that works better, while preserving the roles of the state and CCP.

Critics who claimed that market-led economic reforms would inevitably undermine the state and the CCP have been comprehensively refuted: the Chinese state and CCP are now by most measures stronger than they were 10 or 20 years ago. In the same way, we believe that the critics who believe that governance reform without democracy is doomed to failure will also be refuted, for a while anyway. Our bet is that by 2020 China will have essentially the same political system as it does today, with a well-funded government that delivers greatly improved standards of health, education and environmental protection than today, with a higher general level of administrative professionalism and competence, and possibly (though here we are stretching quite a bit) even with a lower level of corruption. The principal economic consequence of this evolution is that capital and transaction costs throughout the economy will be significantly higher than today.

Given the limits of our readers' patience, which has already been heavily taxed, we offer only the briefest sketch of how governance reform is likely to play out, followed by a few comments on the most egregious misunderstandings of the program. We will accomplish the first by decoding three of the major slogans that president Hu Jintao has issued: "harmonious society" (*hexie shehui*), "scientific concept of development" (*kexue fazhan guan*), and "intraparty democracy" (*dangnei minzhu*).

1. "Harmonious society" is an ingenious formulation that encompasses several ideas. The core idea is that the ideal state of society is cooperation not competition or conflict. In a vague way this resonates with traditional Confucian notions of state, society and the relationship between individuals and institutions. It clearly implies that the state has an obligation to take care of its people, and therefore provides an important ideological mechanism to regulate the behavior of officials. Communist rectitude–summed up in Mao's slogan "serve the people"–has proven bankrupt; so it will now be replaced with a neo-Confucian rectitude whose mantra is "take care of the people." The concrete consequence of this is that officials who cannot show that they have taken care of their subjects in specific ways are unlikely to be promoted.

Correspondingly, individuals have an obligation not to disrupt the harmony of society, e.g. by fomenting political challenges to the ruling elite. In essence, what the harmonious society rubric aims to do is to replace the rather frail social compact of the post-Tiananmen era–get rich and shut up–with a more durable contract in which the government promises a well-ordered society with a rising standard of living; better health, education and social welfare provisions; and more responsiveness to grievances, in exchange for political obedience.

Probably the most important aspect of the harmonious society concept is that it is all about *obligations* and *responsibilities,* and says nothing at all about *rights.* Unlike the West's, China's political language does not include a well-developed way of talking about rights. One can be reasonably sure that the CCP will try to keep it that way. So long as the government has the fiscal resources to deliver steadily greater social services–which it clearly does–and has a mechanism for ensuring that, on balance, officials deliver those services to a greater extent than they are lining their own pockets, then this social compact has a good chance of lasting for the next 15 years.

2. "The scientific concept of development" is essentially the Chinese phrase for what Westerners would call "sustainable development." Implicit in it is the recognition that China's growth model of the economic reform era, which depended on low capital and transaction costs, cannot be continued indefinitely into the future, because of the strains placed on the environment, the escalating cost of resources, and the hidden costs to the state-run banking system that has financed this growth on easy terms.

We believe that one of the least understood aspects of Chinese policy is the extent to which political will has developed at the top of the system to deal not only with China's domestic environmental mess but also with China's contribution to the global problem of climate change. Never mind the stories about the ineffectiveness of the State Environmental Protection Administration (SEPA), true as they are. The bigger story is that by the beginning of 2007, four of the five vice-commissioners of the powerful National Development and Reform Commission (NDRC) had energy efficiency and environment as their areas of focus. One of them, Xie Zhenhua, is a former environment minister, and he remains in place even as some of the other vice-commissioners have been shuffled off to other posts. A restructuring of government ministries in March saw the environmental agency elevated to ministerial status.

The point of all this is simply that environmental and energy-efficiency issues–which Chinese officials view as two sides of the same coin–have moved from the periphery to the center of the economic policy process. Moreover, the solutions to these problems have more to do with governance than with economic management because effective solutions depend on creating more comprehensive systems of accountability for local officials.

This is an important secular shift and in the long run will do much to raise capital costs for industry. But we do not argue that China's huge environmental problems will be easy to solve. Much needs to be done to create effective implementation mechanisms for environmental and energy policies and this is the work of decades.

3. Finally, "intra-party democracy." This is certainly not democracy as anyone outside of China would define it. This idea does, however, encompass a range of measures aimed at the following goals:

- Improving the professional competence of government officials at all levels.

- Improving flows of information within the government, so that the government can identify and respond to problems more quickly.

- Reducing corruption.

The main mechanisms for achieving these goals (all of which have begun to be implemented with increasing rigor) are:

- Stable leadership succession at the top, with succession determined by consensus rather than by one leader picking his successor;

- More consensus-driven decision making at all levels;

- Rules and norms such as age limits, term limits, avoidance of serving in one's home province, and rotation, which aim to limit corruption and the growth of predatory local elites;

- Greater professionalization of the bureaucracy through domestic and international training programs.

One final point. We have elucidated our argument through slogans coined during the Hu Jintao years, but we do not believe that the shift from economic to governance reform was engineered solely by Hu. Rather his slogans codify and attempt to consolidate a consensus among the party elite that has emerged over the past several years. Hu is not a creative political genius like Deng Xiaoping, but a smart yet cautious technocrat operating in an environment where the room for maneuver for an individual leader is far more constrained by Party norms and procedures than was the case in Deng's day. The shift to a governance focus does not, therefore, depend on Hu's personal authority or charisma. When he retires from most or all of his Party and government positions, as we expect he will do by March 2013, there is unlikely to be any substantial shift in the governing consensus.

The one way in which Hu personally does have a major impact is through the personnel system, over which he exercises considerable authority. And here his stamp is quite recognizable. Less than a decade ago, virtually all the members of the Politburo–the approximately

25-person body that is the core center of power in Beijing–had been trained as engineers; the vast majority of provincial chiefs were also engineers. Of the 10 new members elevated to the Politburo last October, only two had engineering degrees. Of the 25 or so provincial bosses (governors and party secretaries) appointed by Hu Jintao over the past five years, only one has an engineering background. Hu's appointees have diverse educational backgrounds, in economics, history, law and politics. Moreover, recent promotions make clear that it is no longer possible to rise to the summit of the Chinese political system–the nine-member Politburo Standing Committee–in the way that Hu Jintao himself did: by spending virtually an entire career prowling the corridors of power in Beijing. To reach the top one must have demonstrated administrative and political competence as an executive at the provincial level.

The message is clear: to get ahead today in the Chinese bureaucracy, political and governance skills matter more than construction skills. This signals that the paramount tasks of the next decade or two are essentially political, not economic in nature.

For as long as we have been visiting China, a chorus of voices has said something like: "The progress of the past 10 years has been impressive, but the problems of the next 10 years will be far more difficult and cannot possibly be solved unless there is *fundamental change* in the political or economic structure." And for the last 23 years the chorus has been proved wrong. How much of a track record is required before this inane formulation is driven to the extinction it richly deserves?

Unfortunately, it is always possible for fundamentalists of various stripes to gain a hearing by confidently declaring that complex problems can be solved by waving a magic wand called "markets" or "democracy." Chinese policymakers ignore the sorcerers and stick to a pragmatic formula: when something works they do more of it, when it doesn't work they stop doing it. Mainly this argues for incrementalism, but occasionally bolder steps are taken. Three recent examples of big things that weren't working and were therefore abandoned were the old state-owned enterprise system, which in 1998 began to be dismantled in favor of the leaner SOE system of today; employer-allocated housing (ended in 2000, to the great benefit of the commercial real estate market) and the once-sacred US-dollar peg of the currency, which was jettisoned in 2005.

The most important point is that a vast number of incremental moves on many fronts can, over a sufficient long period, generate fundamental change. Fifteen years ago, most urban Chinese got assigned jobs by the state right out of school, worked for the state, got their houses from the state, and didn't own property. Today, most urban Chinese find their own jobs, work in the private sector, and own property. The only thing that hasn't changed is that the CCP still monopolizes political power. But the Party has changed too: 15 years ago, ultimate power was wielded in secret by a group of 80-year-old revolutionary leaders who held no formal titles but told the title-holders what to do. Since then there have been two peaceful transitions of leadership at the top, leaders are forced to retire at the age of 70 and lose virtually all of their policy influence when they do so, and no leader is allowed to pick his own successor. That may not be "fundamental" enough change for some, but it is certainly significant change.

It is our belief that anyone who bets against further such significant changes in the structure and style of Chinese governance over the next 15 years is playing a very poor hand, and would do better to throw it in.

How Dependent is China on US Demand?

For much of the past year we have reassured readers that China need not fear a slowdown or recession in the US economy. However, now that US recession fears are growing, and Chinese exports to the US are slowing sharply, should we not start to worry? Not really. Net exports, it is always worth remembering, are **the icing on the Chinese economic cake.** Depending on external demand, the layer of icing may be thicker or thinner. But the cake itself—the size of which is determined by domestic investment—does not change much when some of the icing is scraped off.

We have little doubt that China is about to experience a significant slowdown in export growth. As the chart on the following page shows, there has been a marked downtrend in export growth since late last year, interrupted by a spike in June/July. This spike has clearly been the result of exporters pushing up orders to beat eliminations of VAT rebates on some export products. It is also clear that the rebate cuts have trimmed the exports whose sole purpose was to claim a VAT rebate on imported inputs. Steel exports, for instance, tumbled by nearly 40% from an April high of 7.1m tons to just 4.4m tons in September.

It is also clear that export growth to the US is slowing sharply.

Anecdotal reports further suggest that orders from the US coming to east and south China exporters are weak; though thus far, this has not heavily damaged overall export growth, mainly because the dollar value of exports to Europe has risen steeply.

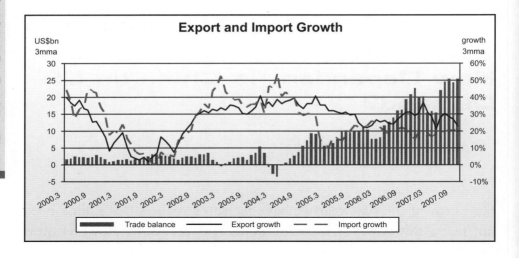

Export and Import Growth

US$bn
3mma

growth
3mma

Legend: Trade balance — Export growth — — Import growth

Chinese export growth by quarter, 2007 % yoy growth

	All	to US
Q1	27.8	20.4
Q2	27.4	15.6
Q3	26.2	12.4

Nevertheless, if one-third of the apparent increase in China's exports to Europe simply represents the higher value of the Euro, volume increases still account for two-thirds. Thus, if US demand continues to weaken and European demand slumps next year (our core scenario), then China's export growth will surely slow. Moreover, as the next chart shows, China's export growth has historically correlated strongly to US GDP growth. We expect this relationship to continue, so a slowdown in the US almost certainly portends a slowdown in Chinese exports. Evidence of this new trend appeared in the October trade data, as export growth fell to 22.2%, or well below the previous quarter's growth rate. Exports also grew less than imports, +25.5% for the first time since January 2006.

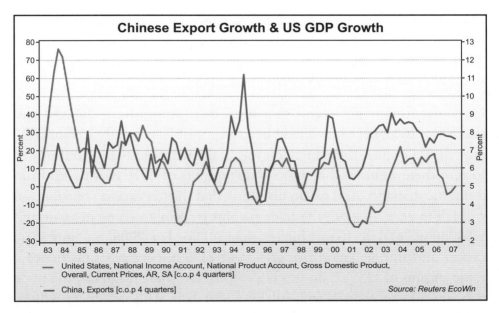

So will the export slowdown lead to a serious slowdown in Chinese GDP growth? A slowdown? Yes! A serious slowdown? No! Indeed, as the chart below shows, there is no particular historical correlation between export growth and GDP growth in China:

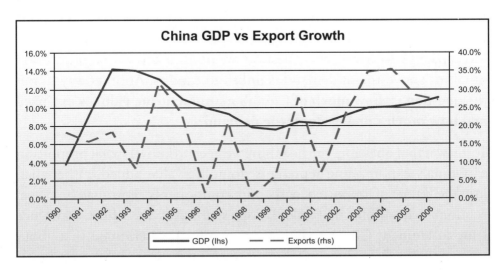

The reason is that China's economy, contrary to popular wisdom, is not export driven but investment driven. Indeed, between 1991 and 2004, the net exports' share of GDP growth was just 1%; the other 99% of GDP growth came from domestic demand.

Of course, one might object that since then, things have changed and that, since 2005, net exports have been responsible for nearly 20% of GDP growth. Yet even at these higher levels, if the net export contribution fell to zero there would still be more than 9 points of GDP growth left from domestic demand. And we do not think that the net export contribution will fall to zero. In 2007, the trade surplus is likely to come in at around US$280bn (or US$103bn higher than 2006). For 2008, we anticipate export and import growth of 20% and 21% respectively and hence a trade surplus of US$325bn (up US$45bn). On these numbers, the trade contribution to growth will fall by about half. The net effect will be to shave about a point off China's GDP growth. And losing a point off growth is not much to worry about–especially when slower surplus growth will ease international imbalances and reduce upward pressure on the RMB.

However, this does raise the question of whether a slowdown in exports could lead to a slowdown in investment as exporters would need to add less capacity? To answer this question, we need to know what proportion of China's investment demand is linked to exports. Another way to put the question is: **how much of China's manufacturing value is exported and how much satisfies domestic demand?**

To answer that question, the first thing we need to know is what proportion of China's export value represents domestic value added, rather than just the value of imported parts and components. Fortunately, a real economist has done that calculation, sparing us the effort. Lawrence Lau, an eminent China economist at Stanford, determined that about 19% of the top-line value of China's exports represented direct domestic value added.

The second piece of information we need is what proportion of China's economy is manufacturing based? In 2005, the last year for which a detailed breakdown is available, the answer was 33% (this share is probably overstated because the service share of the economy is under-measured, but we will leave that aside for the moment).

Composition of GDP by production, 2005

	Rmb bn	% of total
Manufacturing	6,012	32.7
Other industry	2,725	14.8
Services	7,343	40.0
Agriculture	2,307	12.5

Composition of fixed asset investment, 2006

	% of total
Construction	54.8
Infrastructure	30.8
Real estate	24.0
Manufacturing	28.2
Mining	4.0
Other	12.6

Assuming that the domestic value-added share of exports, and the manufacturing share of GDP are constant, we find that in 2006, the domestic value-added component of exports was US$184bn. This works out to 21% of presumed manufacturing value added for the year. If we further assume that there is a one-to-one correspondence between manufacturing value added and manufacturing investment (supported by manufacturing's roughly equal share of GDP and fixed asset investment, see table above), the ultimate conclusion is that about 7% of Chinese investment is directly linked to export production (i.e. 21% of one-third). That calculation was a bit complicated, so let's repeat the bottom line:

- About 21% of China's manufacturing value is exported.

- Manufacturing accounts for about one-third of GDP value and investment.

- Therefore, about 7% of investment expenditure (21% times one-third) is dependent on exports.

We also need to take account of indirect effects: local manufacturing of parts and components sold to export assemblers, inputs of electric power, and so on. Again, Prof Lau comes to the rescue: he estimates these indirect impacts at 19% of export value, the same as the direct impacts. So taking these into account we may conclude that about 14% of Chinese investment expenditure is export-dependent. **Therefore it takes a seven-point drop in export growth to produce a one-point drop in investment growth. Since investment accounts for about 40% of GDP, a seven-point drop in export growth produces a 0.4% drop in GDP growth, above and beyond the reduction in GDP created by the reduction in net exports.**

In conclusion, we would expect export growth to fall to 20% in 2008, down about -7 percentage points from its Q1-3 growth rate of this year. On the above arithmetic, this implies that Chinese GDP growth will slow to about +10% from the current +11.5%. This is significant, but far from catastrophic. More importantly, the GDP drop attributable to investment—which is what determines the level of Chinese demand for the capital goods and raw materials that make up three-quarters of its imports—is less than half a percentage point.

Overall, the message is that China will almost certainly be able to weather a slowdown in global demand, and that its own demand for investment goods will remain pretty strong.

On the Other Side of China's Export Growth–the US Current Account Deficit

Bringing up China's booming export industry without talking about the other side, namely the US current account deficit, would strike our reader as a glaring oversight. So we feel compelled to once again return to this topic, though we are convinced that more ink and paper have been wasted discussing this very issue then any other. As far as we are concerned, the whole issue of the "unsustainability" of the US current account deficit is a massive waste of time. In fact, it is an issue that liberal guiding-lights David Hume and Adam Smith resolved over two centuries ago.

In arguing for free trade, Hume attacked the "strong jealousy with regard to the balance of trade." Hume explained that a nation's gold supply was ultimately determined by its capacity to produce wealth, not the other way around. A nation that attempted to accumulate gold through a trade surplus would soon find that its gold stocks were rising in relation to the total goods available for sale. That excess of money would cause a general rise in the price of domestic goods (i.e., inflation), making them less appealing to foreign buyers. As long as prices kept rising, demand for exports would fall until the inward flow of gold ceased. As Hume understood two centuries ago, any attempt to manufacture a trade surplus through trade policy was doomed to fail because the flow of money would be self-correcting. Around the same time, Adam Smith also dismissed worries about the trade deficit. He wrote, in what remains one of our favorite quotes: "Nothing can be more absurd than this whole doctrine of the balance of trade."

What mattered to Adam Smith (and later David Ricardo) was not the difference between exports and imports but the gains from specialization that trade allows. Those productivity gains allow a nation's residents to produce goods and services of a higher total value--the only true measure of a nation's economic wealth. Any interference in the freedom to trade, no matter what its effect on the trade balance, diminishes that wealth. "A trade which is forced by means of bounties [subsidies] and [protected] monopolies may be, and commonly is, disadvantageous to the country in whose favor it is meant to be established. But that trade which, without force or constraint, is naturally and regularly carried on between any two places, is always advantageous, though not always equally so, to both." And the reality, of course, is that the US current account deficit, and the US' very large trade deficit with China, mostly reflects just such a specialization. It should thus be welcomed rather than bemoaned!

Nevertheless, when we consider global capital flows the really puzzling question is why poor countries such as China or India are saving more than rich ones (the answer, as we tried to show in Chapter 11, is a simple one: poor countries save a lot because they are poor–people there have a lot more to worry about.) And why, to add insult to injury, are they lending their money to the rich instead of investing it in their own countries (where presumably they could earn higher returns)? This is what our friend Brian Reading has called the mystery of "uphill capital flows". There are, we believe, three explanations to this mystery of "uphill capital flows".

The first explanation is that "uphill capital flows" are the direct result of simple mercantilist exchange-rate manipulation. As long as China, Taiwan, Malaysia and other Asian developing countries are determined to prevent their currencies from appreciating against the dollar they will intervene in the FX markets, acquiring dollar reserves. Their capital will continue to flow to America (and, to some degree, Europe) regardless of relative returns. Looking at it this way, we could conclude that the US and Asia are part of a single currency zone and in this sense the imbalances between them are no more a problem than the imbalances within the Eurozone between Germany and Spain (which incidentally are much bigger than the US-Asian imbalances in relation to GDP). Of course if Asian countries decided to drop out of the dollar zone, they would stop buying dollars. But then their currencies would appreciate, automatically reducing the current account imbalances and therefore the need for capital flows. This would essentially be a self-equilibrating process.

The second explanation is that global growth is moving from developed economies to emerging markets—at its simplest because three billion new capitalists are joining the world trading system. But profits are not migrating to emerging markets nearly as fast as output. The Platform Company effect which we have described in detail in our book _Our Brave New World_ means that more and more production happens in places like China, but profits are still earned in the US and Europe, though possibly booked in Bermuda or the Caymans. When Dell sells a $800 computer in America, this counts as an import from China, but US companies make something like $200 profit, while the Chinese manufacturers would be lucky to keep $50. Because production costs are properly registered in official figures, while profits and value added are not, a large part of the US current account deficit is probably an illusion. In effect, the true imbalances are not $800 billion a year as reported in the statistics, but some much smaller number. This means in turn that the US is not really borrowing $800 billion every year from other countries. This observation is consistent with the fact that the US net foreign debt is today much smaller than the accumulated current account deficits of the past 20 years—in fact the difference is well over one trillion dollars.

The third explanation is that emerging market wealth is accumulating in areas of high political risk and weak property rights. In fact, uncertainty of ownership is probably the biggest risk now facing savers in emerging markets. Add to this the fact that Third World capital markets are still somewhat inefficient and emerging market capital will tend to flow naturally to countries with the strongest property rights, greatest political stability and most efficient capital markets. When we ask our clients in

Sao Paolo where the top-end property that rich Brazilians like to buy is located, we tend to always get the same answer: Miami. The same is true of bonds with the highest-quality signatures—i.e. US, Germany or Britain, or hedge funds run out of London or New York. In other words, some investors are willing to accept low financial returns in exchange for political stability and secure ownership rights. This preference for high safety rather than high returns is very natural and rational among emerging market investors, the bulk of whose wealth is trapped in business assets located in high-risk/high-return regions.

This phenomenon helps explains another enigma of the US deficits and current accounts: How is it that the US now has a net foreign debt of $2.5 trillion (blue line, LHS), while it still earns a positive net income of nearly $50 billion (red line, RHS) from these "negative" foreign assets? **In other words, the world's "largest debtor" actually runs a positive cash flow on its debt! So much for the unsustainability of US indebtedness, for whoever heard of anyone going bust with a positive cash flow!**

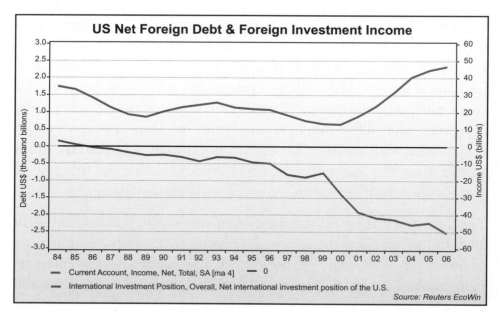

The explanation of this paradox is quite simple: the US earns a much higher rate of return on the assets it owns abroad (roughly 80% of which are either equities or corporate direct investments) than it pays to foreigners on their US assets (which are mostly bonds and bank deposits).

It is often said at this point that the US is behaving like a gigantic hedge fund—with the implication that Americans are running some kind of huge and unquantifiable risk. But the reality is that the US economy is doing something far less glamorous. The US is operating simply like a traditional, mundane commercial bank. The bank takes in money from people who are worried about safety and don't have the connections or the skills to invest it, and then invests these deposits in projects with relatively higher rates of return. In return for the safety it offers and for its skill in assessing credit risks, the bank makes a good profit—incidentally banking has always been a profitable business in every civilization going back to ancient Egypt, China or Mesopotamia. The US today is acting as a banker to the world, especially to the emerging markets and Asia, and is being rewarded for this service (this is even more true, incidentally, of the UK).

To the extent that Middle Eastern investors cannot rely on America to provide them with security of ownership, the shift in global surpluses from Asia to the energy-producing countries helps to explain why the dollar got weaker and the Euro/GBP/CHF stronger as the oil price rose. Note also that this analysis suggests the two truly bearish scenarios for the dollar which we can imagine:

1. The first big risk to the dollar is not that foreigners will lose their appetite for US assets, but that Americans will refuse to sell any more of their assets to foreigners.

2. The second big risk to the dollar is that foreigners no longer trust that their assets will be safe in US banks.

In recent years, both of these risks have been on the rise. And, of course, the US$ has suffered in consequence.

Nevertheless, almost all economists and policymaking institutions—the Fed, the IMF, the OECD—absolutely agree on the fact that, even if the

US deficits were perfectly harmless or even desirable (and remember Adam Smith's quote from above that *"nothing can be more absurd than this whole doctrine of the balance of trade"*), the US current account deficit would soon have to be narrowed, because borrowing $800 billion a year is simply unsustainable and that today, these deficits present the biggest risk to our system.

But, very immodestly, we believe that all these distinguished experts are exactly wrong.

Indeed, while we cannot be sure whether the present US trade deficits are a good or a bad thing; **we have no doubt as to their sustainability.** Deficits of US$800 billion are perfectly sustainable, not just for many more years and decades but, if necessary, forever. This is a matter of simple and irrefutable arithmetic.

A deficit of $800 billion is a very large number, so we have to put it into some kind of perspective. The standard approach is to compare it with GDP. So we say that America's $800 billion deficit is roughly 7% of its $12 trillion GDP—and this sounds pretty scary because anyone can quickly calculate that 15 years of borrowing at this rate would add up to 100% of GDP. In other words, after 15 years of such deficits, the whole American economy would be in hock. Or would it?

The answer, of course, is a very firm no. The reason is that GDP is not the right factor for scaling the deficits on current account. And even though all economists, the IMF, the OECD... do it, it still does not make it right! Comparing deficits to GDP is simply wrong.

The US current account deficit is a mirror image of a capital inflow, or to put it more emotively, the US trade deficits reflect a country living beyond its means by borrowing from foreigners and selling off national assets. Let's be even more insulting: America is selling $800 billion worth of family silver every year to finance its shopaholic addiction (Buffett's share-cropper society). Eventually this rake's progress will surely lead to national bankruptcy, but just when?

To see how long the present rate of borrowing can continue, we should compare the $800 billion America raises each year from Asian pawnbrokers and Middle-Eastern loan sharks with the total amount of family silver it has left to mortgage, sell or pawn. You may think that this wealth is roughly equal to America's national income of $12 trillion, but you would be completely wrong.

The US is one of the few countries in the world which publishes a detailed balance sheet of national wealth, produced quarterly in the Fed's flow of funds statistics. From this we find that the total assets belonging to the US private sector, net of all government and borrowing, both domestic and foreign, is not $12 trillion but $52 trillion. Gross assets (before netting out household debts and the $2 trillion owed to foreigners) are $65 billion. This figure consists of tangible wealth (mostly housing) worth $26 trillion, equity in quoted companies worth $15 trillion, other financial corporate assets (such as bonds and deposits which also represent part of the net worth of the business sector) of roughly $9 trillion plus $15 trillion of "other" assets, much of it represented by the value of national infrastructure plus the net worth of private non-quoted businesses.

Offset against these $65 trillion gross assets are gross liabilities of $12 trillion, three-quarters of which are accounted by mortgage debts (incidentally the assets and liabilities of the corporate sectors and the US government are cancelled out in these calculations, since the net value of companies ultimately belongs to their shareholders in the household sector, while the financial liabilities of the US government are equal to the government assets held by US households and the overseas sector).

If we accept this official estimate of America's wealth (and we have no reason to discard the Fed's data; the reasonableness of the Fed figures is suggested by a back-of-the-envelope calculation: suppose that there are roughly 100 million households living in America and that the average house price is roughly $200,000. Then the total gross value of the US housing stock is around $20 trillion, which is very close to the official figure of $19.8 trillion), then our perspective on the current account deficit is completely changed. Instead of saying that the deficit is 7% of GDP or national income, we should say it is roughly 1.2% of US assets. Instead of describing America's net foreign debt of $2.5 trillion as a scary 20% of national income, we can more meaningfully express it as 4% of national net worth.

Much more importantly, America's $52 trillion net worth is not a static figure. Both net and gross wealth in America have been growing by a steady 5-6% in nominal terms every year since 1955. This means that the US net worth is growing by roughly $3 trillion each year, while it borrows $800 billion from the rest of the world. In other words, the US is not exactly scraping together the last of its family silver and sentimental heirlooms to finance its consumption binge; rather it is selling (or more precisely mortgaging) between one-quarter and one-third of the annual growth in its net worth.

Now let us put America's supposed national profligacy into the context of a corporate business. Suppose you were analyzing a company with a turnover of $11 billion, a net worth of $54 billion and $2.5 billion of net debt. And suppose that its shareholders' funds were growing steadily by $3 billion each year. This company comes to you and says that it wants to increase its leverage by borrowing $800 million a year. What would you do? You might ask the management whether it had good projects in which to deploy this extra cash. You might ask whether the borrowing program would increase or reduce its long-term RoE. You might wonder whether the company should be even more aggressively or more conservatively managed. But one thing you would not dream of asking is whether this company was about to go bankrupt—remember it is borrowing $800 million on the basis of $54 billion net equity and an annual increase of $3 billion in net worth!

You might, however, note that by adding $800 million each year to a debt, which begins at only $2.5 billion, the company will be steadily increasing its debt-to-equity ratio. Given that this debt equity ratio starts at only 4% this would hardly be an immediate worry, but you might, out of pure curiosity, wonder how many years (or decades) the company could keep up this rate of borrowing before the debt-equity ratio started to draw attention from Moody's and S&P. To do this, you would run a spreadsheet which analyzed what would happen to the various financial ratios if the initial rate of borrowing continued for many years ahead.

This is exactly what we can do for the US. Let us start with a debt-to-asset ratio of 4% and with both GDP and gross wealth growing at a steady 6% per annum. Let us assume that the current account deficit begins at $800 billion and then, far from returning to balance, keeps getting bigger at the same rate as GDP growth (i.e. 6% per annum). The results are summarized in the chart below.

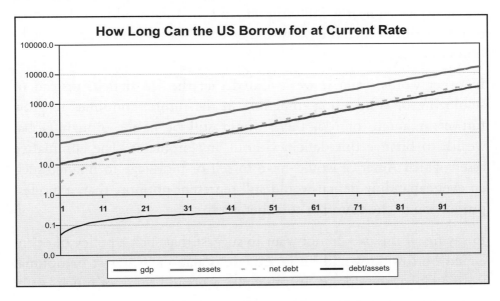

The scale on the left is trillions of dollars–the initial foreign debt is $2.5 trillion, GDP is $11 trillion, US net wealth is $54 trillion and time is shown in years from the starting point. The red line at the bottom shows the ratio of foreign debt to net assets.

What we find is that the US could afford to borrow $800 billion–and continue borrowing this amount, increasing amount rising by 6%

annually—forever without its foreign debt to asset ratio ever exceeding 26%. In the first few decades of this foreign borrowing program, the debt-to-asset ratio would rise gradually from an initial 10%, to 13% after 10 years, 19% after 20 years, and 22% after 30 years. After that the growth in the debt-equity ratio would gradually tail off, until it stabilized at around 25% after 40 years. By that time, US net foreign debt would be over $100 trillion and the current account deficit would be $8 trillion a year.

These astronomical numbers may sound utterly impossible, but all they really show us about is the magic of compound interest, rather than unsustainable profligacy. By 2045, when on present trends the US foreign debt would reach $100 trillion, the net wealth of the US private sector would be nearly $500 trillion—and the total wealth of the global economy from which the US would be borrowing would be five to eight times as large.

In other words, even if we assumed that the US deficit, instead of stabilizing or contracting sometime in the future, continues to grow forever at a rate of 6%, there would still be easily enough global wealth to finance this deficit without any problems. The cumulative assets which America would have to sell or mortgage to finance such an ever-expanding deficit would still represent no more than a modest proportion of the country's total net worth.

In saying all this, we do not want to suggest that such a policy of open-ended borrowing would be in America's national interest or optimal from a global standpoint. In principle, we could think of much better alternatives to the present global imbalances.

For example, we would prefer to see a much more expansionary monetary and fiscal policy in Europe. We would also like to see higher exchange rates in Japan, China and rest of Asia (more on that later). And we would love to see much lower oil prices, with OPEC producers and Russia forced by WTO rules to offer unlimited production licenses to Exxon, Shell, Total, BP and other Western producers. But none of these blessings seems very likely in the near future. And until this Golden Age dawns, we must return to the question of whether the US current account deficit is unsustainable.

Most dismal scientists would tell us that a situation in which the Western world consumes, through increasing leverage while emerging markets (especially Asia) produce, is not 'sustainable'. In fact, we are told that the large US trade deficits will one day lead to a 'US$ crisis', a refusal by foreigners to finance US consumption, etc…

To illustrate what is wrong about how economists view the world, and how the above view has little resemblance with reality, consider the following example: Let us assume that a Dell PC sells in the US for US$700. Now let's have a look at how this very simple transaction is recorded in a) Accounting 101 and in b) Economics 101.

Accounting 101:

The flat screen, built in Taiwan, costs US$300. The margin of the Taiwanese manufacturer is US$30. The mechanical part and the box, built in China, cost US$100, with a margin of US$5. The Intel chip (designed in the US but made by TSMC in Taiwan) cost US$70 with a margin of US$35 going back to Intel and US$5 going to TSMC. The Microsoft software cost US$200, with a margin of 90%, or US$180. Dell tacks on a US$30 profit for selling the PC.

Profits for the US economy: US$35 (Intel) + US$180 (MSFT) + US$30 (Dell) = US$245

Profits for foreign economies: US$30 (Taiwanese flat screen maker) + US$5 (TSMC) + US$5 (Chinese assembly line) = US$40

Difference: +US$205 on behalf of US companies

Conclusion: this looks like a good deal all around for the US: the US consumer gets a cheap PC and US companies capture most of the profits in the process. On an accounting basis, everything looks rosy…

Now let's see how an economist views the above transactions.

Economics 101

Imports: US$470 (price of the PC minus the Dell mark-up and Microsoft software); Exports: US$0

Trade Deficit= US$470.

Increase in GDP, due to Microsoft, Dell and Intel profits = US$245

Net loss for the US economy, US$ 470-US$245 = -US$225

Conclusion drawn by the economists: this is a really unsustainable situation. The US economy is moving more and more in debt to foreigners who one day could decide not to sell in the US anymore, leading to a collapse in the US$, a rise in US interest rates, etc....

But in the real world, is this situation really unsustainable? Absolutely not!

What is unsustainable is measuring global trade flows in terms of *sales*, without looking at *profits* - which is what trade numbers do–and deriving investment implications from these measures. If the fellows exporting to the US make on average a margin of 1%, while US exporters churn out margins of 20%, then, which economy would you rather own? Economists assume that, over time, imports and exports have to balance, otherwise a country moves into debt. And then, one day the music stops and 'it is time to pay up!' This simple, Calvinist, idea would be true if margins on imports and margins on exports were the same, but this is simply never the case. And it is increasingly less so; if anything, margins have been diverging, not converging.

Trade balances are computed on sales. Implicit in this computation are two hypotheses:

a) that the margins on imports and exports are the same, and

b) that sales must balance each other over the long term.

But these assumptions are so stupid that only an economist could make them. Indeed, instead of having sales balance off each other over the long term, goods (as we have tried to show above) can be exchanged for assets. So the so-called 'US debt to the outside world' can be easily repaid by the sale of US assets to foreigners. And this does not mean that the US gets poorer over time (i.e., the share-cropper society of Mr Buffett), unless of course one wants to assume that the stock of US assets is fixed and does not grow (a silly assumption to make).

Consider the following: companies in the US have very stable and robust earnings. In the previous example, US companies had profits of US$245/US$700. Now let us imagine that, in the stock market, these earnings are capitalised at 20x on average. This gives a market cap of US$4,900 per computer sold. And then we get to the all-important question: will the Chinese/Taiwanese savers (who sold a PC to the US and so received US$) prefer to buy the assets of their own country? Or those of the United States? Obviously, everything depends on relative prices; but at equal prices, the Chinese savers will want to be invested in the 'safer' US assets (if given the choice).

Assuming that, in China/Taiwan, salaries represent 50% of sales or US$220, and that the poor factory workers save 50% of their salaries, then the employees can buy US$110 worth of high quality shares in the US, or US$110/US$4,900=2.2%.

If the demand for computers in the US increases by 10%, then the trade deficit will become even bigger, but the poor Chinese worker will still only be able to buy 2.2% of US equities with his gains (since the price of US assets will also rise by 10%). The poor Chinese worker will be chasing a moving target.

Let us leave theory behind and return to the real world. In 1991, foreigners owned 11% of the US stock market. Since 1991, the US stock market (dividends included) has more than quadrupled. Today, after a continued deterioration in the US current account deficit, foreigners own around 17% of the US market. The fact that foreigners increased their holdings in the last 17 years by 50% goes a long way in explaining why the US stock market has quadrupled (since prices are made at the margin). But, at the end of the day, everybody is richer: the US consumer, the owners of US companies, the Chinese companies and the Chinese workers. And as long as the US has assets to sell, then there will be no reason to worry.

The economist Herb Stein famously observed in the 1960s that if something is unsustainable, then sooner or later it stops. What he meant by this was that if you see something happening in practice for many years on end, then there is no point in arguing that it is impossible as a matter of theory. But strangely enough, most economists these days present this maxim the other way round. They say that deficits of 8% of GDP are obviously unsustainable, and therefore they will have to stop sooner or later. This is simply untrue. For the past 20 years, US trade deficits have been consistently growing, and have consistently been denounced as irresponsible and unsustainable. Yet the same 20 years have seen unprecedented economic stability and accelerating global growth.

Throughout these 20 years the US, Britain and other deficit countries have consistently shown better economic performance than Japan, Germany, Saudi Arabia and other economies with large surpluses. This experience inspires two opposing conclusions: either you can start from the theory that deficits are unsustainable and harmful and conclude from this that the US or other deficit economies are getting steadily weaker while the global financial system is becoming chronically unstable. Or you can start from the empirical facts—that deficit economies have performed better than ever in the past 20 years and note that the global financial system has been remarkably stable, despite numerous shocks (9/11, Iraq War, Enron, oil at US$70, Katrina, Refco, GM downgrade…). You can then conclude that the theory of unsustainable deficits must simply be wrong.

You have to be awfully confident in your theories to believe that they represent reality, while 20 years of continuous experience is just a fleeting mirage.

The Platform Company Business Model: How Globalization Changed the Structure of Successful Companies

As Adam Smith pointed out in *The Wealth of Nations*, what mattered to a nation's wealth was specialization in the industry where one had the greatest absolute advantages. Ricardo then showed that what actually mattered were comparative advantages (i.e., if France is good at producing wine and Senegal is good at producing world-class football players, then France should produce wine and Senegalese should play on the French football team ... or something like that).

And today, it seems obvious that almost the whole world (apart from President Sarkozy and large segments of the US Democratic Party) has finally accepted this premise. No one sits around wondering whether to build textile plants in North Carolina or Lille. Instead, it is an accepted fact that textiles will from now on be produced somewhere in Asia, North Africa or Central America.

Now with that in mind, it may be useful to review what companies have historically done. Up until recently, a typical company designed a product, manufactured the product, and then sold the product. Take Ford as an example. Ford designs an Expedition SUV. Ford manufactures the truck at a plant in Detroit. Ford then sends the truck on to a Ford dealership somewhere in the US to be sold. This vertical design/produce/sell business model has been the model de rigueur for the past 50 years. Really successful companies followed this model at home, then abroad (i.e., Toyota). Companies became multinationals. Each multinational started as a purely domestic company, and eventually started to produce everywhere to sell wherever they were producing.

This was yesterday's business model.

The new business model is to produce nowhere, but sell everywhere. In recent years, we have witnessed the birth of a new breed of company that we have called 'platform companies'. Platform companies know where the clients are and what they want and where the producers are. Platform companies then simply organize the ordering by the clients and the delivery by the producers (and the placing of their logo on the product just before delivery).

Platform companies keep the high added-value parts of research, development, treasury and marketing in-house, and farm out all the rest to external producers. Typical examples include Apple, Dell, Ikea, Hennes & Mauritz, Esprit, Li and Fung and so many others…

Indeed, an increasing number of Western companies are looking at their business models and saying: 'Out of the three things I do–designing, producing and selling–producing is a mug's game. Producing ties up a lot of capital. It is often labour-intensive. It forces me to keep expensive inventories. It is highly volatile. And I do not get rewarded for it in the marketplace (manufacturing businesses typically trade at discounts to non-manufacturing businesses in the stock market, mostly because they are more volatile, and offer lower returns on invested capital). I would be better off leaving the producing to some other mug, and focus on the non-cyclical, high value-added part of my business, namely designing and selling.'

An increasing number of companies have taken a look at their operations and decided that the way to succeed was to operate on much leaner balance sheets. Take hotel companies as an example. Apart from Accor of France, most hotel companies around the world (Hilton, Marriott, etc.) have, or are trying, to shed assets. Instead of owning hotels, they simply manage them.

In micro-economic terms, this 'light balance sheet' model makes plenty of sense. It allows companies to act swiftly if/when a decision has been wrong. It is like travelling with a small backpack instead of travelling with a suite of trunks. One can change itineraries rapidly and avoid losses. When executed properly, the 'platform company' business model makes for very high, and stable, returns on invested capital.

Of course, this new business model also has important economic, political, social and financial implications...all of which we attempted to deal with in our book *Our Brave New World* though, at the risk of "re-heating" some old material, we would like to highlight the most important consequence of the growth of platform companies, namely the drop in volatility and the growth in profitability.

Indeed, as Western companies adopt the 'platform-company' model, and outsource the 'manufacturing' tasks, Western economies shed industrial jobs.

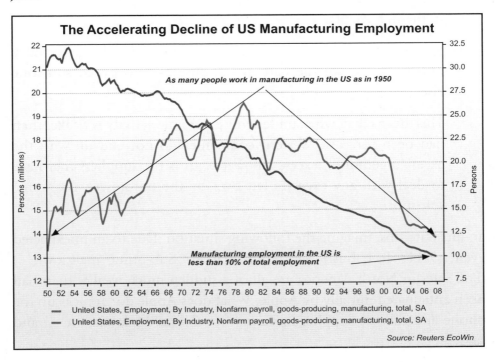

In fact, countries like the US have lost so many industrial jobs in recent years (witness the drop between 2000 and 2004) that we should probably stop calling Western nations 'industrialized nations'. Western countries are increasingly anything but industrialized! Today, industry is in China, Poland, Korea, Mexico... Meanwhile economies like the US, the UK, the Netherlands should be called Western post-industrial nations, or Western service economies...

Needless to say, the loss of industrial jobs is a disaster for industrial workers; and for politicians whose efforts depend on large pools of organized labor (which may explain why the US Democratic Party has turned increasingly against free-trade in recent years). But unless one is an industrial worker, a trade union, or a democratic politician this is great news. Why? Because it means that the underlying economy loses most of its cyclicality. Let us explain:

- The industrial part of the production process is by far the most cyclical of the three step (design, produce, sell) process described in the first chapter.

- So as companies outsource the 'production' part, they effectively outsource the volatile part of the business process to someone else.

- This means that, when underlying economic activity is weaker than had been forecast, Western companies do not end up with the excess inventories, excess labor etc... It is the suppliers that have to deal with any excesses left over by the unforeseen economic soft-spot.

To illustrate this, imagine the following situation. Due to an unexpected event (9/11? Tech bust? Very cold weather? Sub-prime meltdown...) iPod sales in North America are all of a sudden much weaker than had been anticipated initially by Apple. What does Apple do? It picks up the phone and calls its supplier in Taiwan (or China, Malaysia, etc...) and says:

Apple: 'Sorry. I know that, this time last year, we ordered 350,000 iPods from you. But this month, we will only need 50,000.

Supplier: 'But I have already bought the PCB and LCD for 350,000 iPods!'

Apple: 'Really? Then I guess you can give me a special deal on the 50,000 iPods that I do need. After all, you will want to get rid of your inventories.'

Supplier: 'But how am I supposed to make my employee payrolls?'

Apple: 'Sorry my friend. There are two kinds of problems in the capitalist world in which we live: mine, and not mine. Your inventory, and payroll issues, is the second kind of problem'.

Because of the slowdown in the demand for iPods, the supplier in Taiwan (or elsewhere) is then forced to lay off people. Meanwhile, the designers at Apple are hard at work on finding new designs which will draw people back into the stores, as are the Apple marketing teams. In neither of the latter two activities do we witness massive lay-offs. Apple's people in the United States remain duly employed.

In a downturn, industrial workers always get the cull first. And as industrial workers are fired, their consumption falls, thereby forcing the next manufacturer to cut jobs etc... This is how we sometimes enter into a recessionary spiral. But now, industrial workers are abroad. Which means that, in a downturn, lay-offs are mild compared to previous cycles, as are the swings in overall economic activity.

To put it another way, when the Western economies were highly industrialized, the variable of adjustments for the economic cycle were either profits or employment; when the labor market was tight, companies would retain workers and take any adjustment on their bottom line and when the labour market was loose, companies would try to maintain their profitability and fire workers. But today, with services gaining an ever important piece of the economic pie, the variable of adjustment for Western economies is no longer employment, or profits. It is imports.

Look at what has happened to US economic aggregates in recent years.

First the volatility of industrial production shrank as companies started to outsource the most volatile, or capital intensive, part of their production process.

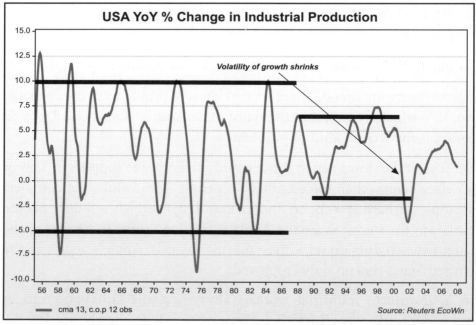

USA YoY % Change in Industrial Production

Volatility of growth shrinks

cma 13, c.o.p 12 obs

Source: Reuters EcoWin

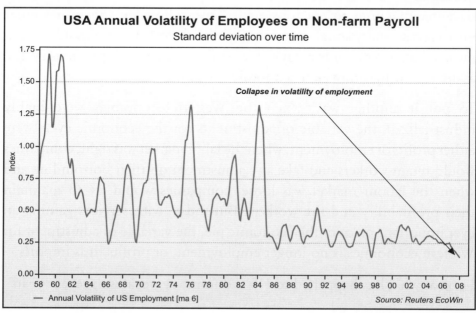

USA Annual Volatility of Employees on Non-farm Payroll

Standard deviation over time

Collapse in volatility of employment

Annual Volatility of US Employment [ma 6]

Source: Reuters EcoWin

Secondly, as more and more workers held non-industrial jobs, the volatility of employment collapsed.

As companies started to adopt the "platform company model", they shifted their investment from capital intensive Property, Plant and Equipment to spending on knowledge, branding and distribution. In turn, this had two effects. First, companies have less capital tied up in expensive, heavy equipment and inventories. Second, companies need less capital to generate a given level of sales and their interest costs have fallen. The following chart shows the proportion of capital non-financial companies have tied up in inventories. Clearly, the trend is down... which is good news since the liquidation of inventories can often lead to abrubpt swings in the economic cycle.

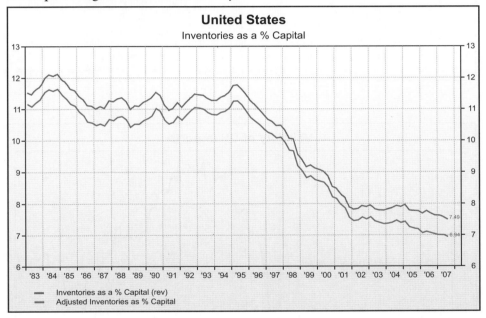

As a result, not only did margins increase, the downside volatility of profits fell.

At the same time, the volatility of US imports rose markedly, especially in the leaner economic growth years (2001-2002) as imports replaced profits and employment as the main variable of adjustment in the economic cycle.

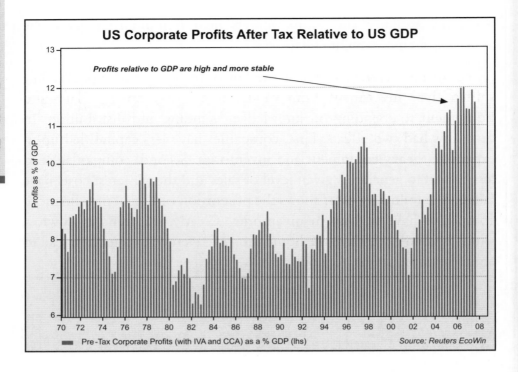

US Corporate Profits After Tax Relative to US GDP

Profits relative to GDP are high and more stable

Profits as % of GDP

Pre-Tax Corporate Profits (with IVA and CCA) as a % GDP (lhs)

Source: Reuters EcoWin

Volatility of US Imports

Steady increase in import volatility over the past decade

Source: Reuters EcoWin

148

So when people claim that, today, all the US does is consume and never exports anything, this is not exactly true. Thanks to the platform companies, the US and other Western economies (after all IKEA is Swedish, Carrefour is French, Li & Fung is from Hong Kong etc...) have managed to export...the volatile part of their economic cycles!

A less volatile economic cycle is, needless to say, a great thing to have. It allows entrepreneurs to plan for the future more consistently, consumers to make decisions for the long term in the knowledge that they will not lose their jobs, governments to plan for fairly accurate tax receipts, companies to paint accurate pictures of future earnings to shareholders, shareholders to take more risk, etc...

Given the deep impact on our economies that this change in business model has triggered, we firmly believe that the past decade's globalization of the structure of global production has been and remains a "Third Structural Mega-Trend". It is the main explanation behind the impressive growth of productivity in the US. And what is capitalism all about if not always trying to produce more with less?

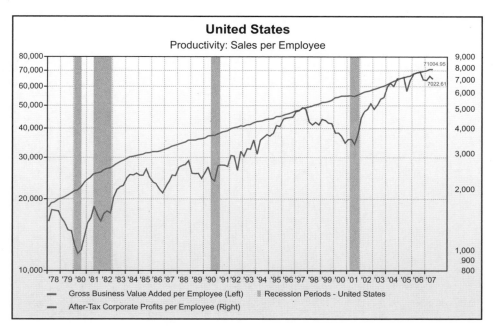

An Era of Accelerating Schumpeterian Growth

Over two centuries ago, Robert Malthus made his dire predictions that the world would soon be unable to support the rapid population growth that he was starting to witness all around him. Malthus, who was an Anglican pastor, not an economist, explained that while the population increased by geometrical progression, resources - particularly agricultural ones - grew arithmetically. Of course, two centuries of experience have shown that this apparently logical notion was false. The Reverend Malthus, despite all his wisdom, did not account for capitalism's two main driving forces: Ricardian growth and Schumpeterian growth. Indeed, when we review capitalism's history of growth and progress, we find that progress has usually come as a result of either:

1. A rational re-organisation of talents. David Ricardo gave the best expression of this source of growth in his law of comparative advantages. Even if a surgeon can type faster than his secretary, if cutting flesh is paid more by the hour than typing letters, the surgeon should hire a secretary to do all of his typing, thereby freeing as much time as possible to cut flesh. This argument is of course most often applied to free trade but it works across any company, region, or economy.

To promote the Ricardian kind of growth, one needs low trade barriers, low regulations and a government that does not interfere in the overall economy. To promote the Schumpeterian kind of growth, one also needs low regulations, low taxes, easy access to capital and, most importantly, the ability and right to fail. These factors have been prevalent, at least across the Western world, for a generation, which helps explain why, over the past twenty years, growth around the World has been so strong and why we live with unprecedented levels of wealth.

Now it could be argued that the three structural trends we highlighted above (the financial revolution, the growth in emerging markets and the rise of the platform company business model) are each some kind of variants of "Ricardian growth". One could also argue that, at some point, this "Ricardian growth" will dry up. After all, one can only eliminate so many inefficiencies through free trade deals; and one can only optimize a balance sheet and a production process up to a point. Fortunately, we are nowhere near that point of maximum efficiency yet (and anyone who doubts that should have to spend a few days in India, the world's second most populous country).

Fortunately, while there may be limits to Ricardian growth at some point in the very distant future, there are no physical limits whatsoever to the second kind of growth, namely Schumpeterian growth.

2. Growth can come from inventions put in place by entrepreneurs. Growth triggered by inventions is a totally different kind of growth altogether. A new invention can trigger new demands, lead to new products, new management techniques and new markets. At the same time, inventions can also lead to the collapse of old products or old firms. This is the 'creative destruction' which Schumpeter described.

By its very nature, there is no limit to the possibilities of Schumpeterian growth. Man will always come up with new inventions. But these inventions can be as destructive as they are creative. This is why Schumpeter called the growth process 'creative destruction'. A quick example: when the fax machine was invented, it spelled the doom of the telex machine (who nowadays has a telex machine in their office?). And when email was invented, the number of faxes sent collapsed…

So how does one promote Schumpeterian growth? We believe that you need at least three very important variables to be in place:

#1: The Right, and the Ability, to Fail

As mentioned above, one man's invention is often another man's ruin; there is a dark side to the force of capitalism. For decades, this dark side of the force has deeply disturbed governments. Firstly, because the dark side appears inhumane. Secondly, because special interest groups threatened by the dark side can be very organised and vociferous (steel industry in the US, construction industry in Japan, farmers and rail workers in France…), bringing to politicians the two things they need: votes & money. Thirdly, because some politicians (namely in continental Europe) think they can control for the greater good, with measures and laws, the might of the dark side.

Unfortunately, more often than not, attempts to reduce the effects of the dark side only end up stifling the creative side of the force. Rather than protect jobs, protectionism, market regulation and other measures to prevent competition typically block future inventions and current growth.

#2- The Legal Protection of Intellectual Property

In the 'Third Wave' society in which we now live, 'value' is increasingly domiciled in intellectual property. Stripped of intellectual property, what would Microsoft be worth? Or Novartis? Or GaveKal? Okay, that last one is probably a stretch since GaveKal is not worth much… but our reader gets the drift. Without a healthy respect for intellectual property, and established legal procedures to defend it, Schumpeterian growth simply can not flourish.

Establishing the legal framework in which intellectual property can flourish is not easy. It is also an everyday task given the constant evolutions in our brave new world; for example, the US Supreme Court recently had to establish the legality, or not, of music file-sharing over the Internet.

Today, intellectual property is decently protected in the Western world but it is not in the greater Emerging Markets. This important difference helps explain, we believe, why so many platform companies are domiciled in the Western world, and so few are in the emerging countries.

This stark difference, however, does not mean that all is rosy for the Western economies, and that good ideas and new processes will only continue to emerge from there. Far from it. In fact, one point of serious concern is that politicians all across the Western world are making the mistakes of their forefathers all over again. Let us explain through the British example.

Following WWII, the British Labour party identified three sectors as the 'growth sectors' of the economy: steel, coal and rail. The government then said that these growth sectors would be better managed by the state. Of course, we know what happened. Today, Britain has no steel, coal or rail industry to speak of. The nationalization of these important sectors prevented ideas from flourishing; creative destruction could not apply.

Today, all over Europe, governments are up to the same trick. While they are happy to leave rail, coal and steel by the side (having destroyed these industries), the new three 'growth' sectors of the future have been identified by governments. They are: education, pensions and healthcare. But in a number of countries, France, Germany, Italy... the governments are saying: these three sectors are the 'chasse-gardée' (protected area) of the government. No-one else is allowed to butt in...

This can only mean two things. Firstly, that capital will be wasted (and because these sectors require increasing amounts of capital, the governments will either take it from the taxpayer, or—more likely—finance it through deficits). Secondly, that the growth of ideas, and the pace of creative destruction, will be unfortunately restrained.

#3- The Acceptance of Income Disparity

More than the above, Schumpeterian growth also needs an acceptance by society of important income disparities. Indeed, what is the point to work hard and put together new inventions if a government takes all profits away in the name of social equality? Any country aiming to promote Schumpeterian growth needs to recognize that the desire to strike it rich remains the greatest motivator. In 1982, Deng Xiaoping announced that 'to get rich is glorious'; since then, the income of China's city dwellers has increased 14x.

This acceptance of income disparity is probably the hardest thing to achieve in the current political structure of most countries. Why? Because most countries oppose the 'social' to the unequal' and strive to avoid wide income disparities.

But the refusal to accept income disparities is a very destructive act. Inherently, it implies that capital is taken from where it is efficient and generating high returns, and distributed where it isn't. Such a course of action can only lead to an impoverishment of the greater society; and when the greater society gets poorer, it is the poorest members who suffer the most. Time and again, this has been the experience of socialism.

Trying to prevent the growth of income disparities is also denying an important economic reality: income disparities are a tremendously creative force. As Thorstein Veblen showed in *The Theory of the Leisure Class,* one of the main motors of capitalism is the desire for conspicuous consumption; or, as popular knowledge calls it, the wish to 'keep up with the Jones'. 'If there are no Jones' to keep up with, why get out of bed in the morning?

Looking around the world today, we find that the economies riding Alvin Toffler's 'third wave' to the limit of its potential all take a benign view of income disparity, whether the US, the UK, Australia, Hong Kong…

Staying on Hong Kong, the city-state surely ranks as one of the greatest success stories of the past fifty years; and no first time visitor to the city fails to be shocked by how vibrant, and wealthy, the city is and the disparities of wealth on display.

Hong Kong's economy was destroyed by the Japanese in WWII, destroyed by the UN embargo on trade against China in 1951, crimpled by worries over the return of the territory to China. Hong Kong has been hit by typhoons, mud-slides, squatter-camp fires, bird flu, SARS and massive refugee influxes. Hong Kong has no mines, no oil wells, very little agriculture. Hong Kong also has nowhere to park; yet, the town has the highest ratio of Rolls Royces, Ferraris and Porsches per capita. And Hong Kong also has one of the lowest rate crime in the world. How did Hong Kong achieve this success? By encouraging wealth disparity. Hong Kong is a city without minimum wage, where the wealthy reap huge rewards.

And yet there is little social tension. Why? Because the unfortunate workers at the bottom of the ladder believe that one day, things will be better. This is a very important point: income disparities are untenable when there is no hope of social advancement. But that is not the case in the US, the UK, Australia, Hong Kong where you find lots of rags to riches stories (i.e., Li Ka Shing). And even more rags to middle class stories.

When the process of creative destruction is allowed to work, we get both income disparity and the ability of people to 'move up'. When income disparity is constrained, the ability of people to climb the social ladder disappears. This is why, in large parts of Europe, the social ladder is missing a few steps...

Nevertheless, before we allow negative thoughts to take hold, we have to acknowledge a profound reality: **we live today in an era of "accelerating creative destruction"!** And this for a simple reason: while the industrial revolution multiplied man's physical strength, the Internet and technology revolutions have multiplied man's intellectual strength. Resources that, until recently, had been locked away in the world's best libraries are now open for all to see–facts and figures that just ten years ago took dozens of hours to gather are now no further than a mouse-click away.

And exchanging ideas on any topic with complete strangers half way around the world who can offer a refreshing and different perspective is something that all of us have grown accustomed to doing on a daily basis. This is one of the many reasons that our economy is so different from the economy of a generation ago.

In their latest book, *Revolutionary Wealth,* Alvin & Heidi Toffler identify ten characteristics which make knowledge a different input to wealth creation altogether. They explain that:

1. Knowledge is inherently non rival: if you use a Microsoft program, it does not mean that there is less for the rest of the world.

2. Knowledge is intangible: We can't touch it or slap it, but we can, and do, manipulate it.

3. Knowledge is non linear: A small breakthrough can lead to huge results.

4. Knowledge is relational: Two apparently separate pieces of knowledge can yield huge results if and when combined.

5. Knowledge mates with other knowledge. Knowledge is very promiscuous and very fertile.

6. Knowledge is more portable than any other product: Once converted to zeros and ones, it can be distributed instantaneously all over the world.

7. Knowledge can be compressed in symbols and abstractions.

8. Knowledge can be stored in smaller and smaller places (including, to my surprise, some of my analysts' heads).

9. Knowledge can be explicit or implicit, expressed or not expressed, shared or tacit. There is no tacit truck.

10. Knowledge is hard to bottle up. It spreads.

Now what is exciting today is that wealth creation is **for the first time in history, result of using something which is in unlimited supply,** and which has a marginal cost of zero. This puts into question the whole intellectual framework on which the science of economics is built (allocating scarcity rationally). Indeed, what is the use of marginal analysis when the marginal cost is zero? The notion of markets is changing in front of our very eyes. A market in which the supply is infinite is not a market. Neither the economists, nor the accountants, nor the analysts have done enough work to understand the implications. What we do know is that the tools to measure or manage a knowledge-based economy will be profoundly different than those necessary to measure an industrial-based economy. It's simply not about allocating scarcity anymore!

Two authors that present this theme in a clear and concise fashion are Don Tapscott and Anthony Williams who together wrote *Wikinomics*, another must read to understand the structural changes that are revolutionizing our economies. And rather than try to explain and distort what is a remarkable thesis, I would rather quote at length (I hope that the authors will not mind):

"It was late in the afternoon, on a typically harsh Canadian winter day, as Rob McEwen, the CEO of Goldcorp Inc., stood at the head of the boardroom table confronting a room full of senior geologists. The news he was about to deliver was not good. In fact it was disastrous, and McEwen was having a hard time shielding his frustration.

The small Toronto-based gold-mining firm was struggling, besieged by strikes, lingering debts, and an exceedingly high cost of production which had caused them to cease mining operations. Conditions in the marketplace were hardly favorable. The gold market was contracting, and most analysts assumed that the company's fifty-year old mine in Red Lake, Ontario, was dying. Without evidence of substantial new gold deposits, the mine seemed destined for closure, and Goldcorp was likely to go down with it.

Tensions were running at a fever pitch. McEwen had no real experience in the extractive industries, let alone in gold mining. Nevertheless, as an adventurous young mutual fund manager he had gotten involved in a takeover battle and emerged as Goldcorp Inc.'s majority owner. Few people in the room had much confidence that McEwen was the right person to rescue the company. But McEwen just shrugged off his critics.

He turned to his geologists and said, "We're going to find more gold on this property, and we won't leave this room tonight until we have a plan to find it." At the conclusion of the meeting he handed his geologists $10 million for further exploration and sent them packing for northern Ontario.

Most of his staff thought he was crazy but they carried out his instructions, drilling in the deepest and most remote parts of the mine. Amazingly, a few weeks later they arrived back at Goldcorp headquarters beaming with pride and bearing a remarkable discovery: Test drilling suggested rich deposits of new gold, as much as thirty times the amount Goldcorp was currently mining!

The discovery was surprising, and could hardly have been better timed. But after years of further exploration, and to McEwen's deep frustration, the company's geologists struggled to provide an accurate estimate of the gold's value and exact location. He desperately needed to inject the urgency of the market into the glacial processes of an old-economy industry.

In 1999, with the future still uncertain, McEwen took some time out for personal development. He wound up at an MIT conference for young presidents when coincidentally the subject of Linux came up. Perched in the lecture hall, McEwen listened intently to the remarkable story of how Linus Torvalds and a loose volunteer brigade of software developers had assembled the world-class computer operating system over the Internet. The lecturer explained how Torvalds revealed his code to the world, allowing thousands of anonymous programmers to vet it and make contributions of their own.

McEwen had an epiphany and sat back in his chair to contemplate. If Goldcorp employees couldn't find the Red Lake gold, maybe someone else could. And maybe the key to finding those people was to open up the exploration process in the same way Torvalds "open sourced" Linux.

McEwen raced back to Toronto to present the idea to his head geologist. "I'd like to take all of our geology, all the data we have that goes back to 1948, and put it into a file and share it with the world," he said. "Then we'll ask the world to tell us where we're going to find the next six million ounces of gold." McEwen saw this as an opportunity to harness some of the best minds in the industry. Perhaps understandably, the in-house geologists were just a little skeptical. Mining is an intensely secretive industry, and apart from the minerals themselves, geological data is the most precious and carefully guarded resource. It's like the Cadbury secret—it's just not something companies go around sharing. Goldcorp employees wondered whether the global community of geologists would respond to Goldcorp's call in the same way that software developers rallied around Linus Torvalds. Moreover, they worried about how the contest would reflect on them and their inability to find the illusive gold deposits.

McEwen acknowledges in retrospect that the strategy was controversial and risky. "We were attacking a fundamental assumption; you simply don't give away proprietary data," he said. "It's so fundamental," he adds, "that no one had ever questioned it." Once again, McEwen was determined to soldier on.

In March 2000, the "Goldcorp Challenge" was launched with a total of $575,000 in prize money available to participants with the best methods and estimates. Every scrap of information (some four hundred megabytes worth) about the 55,000–acre property was revealed on Goldcorp's Web site. News of the contest spread quickly around the Internet, as over one thousand virtual prospectors from fifty countries got busy crunching the data.

Within weeks, submissions from around the world came flooding in to Goldcorp headquarters. As expected, geologists from around the world got involved. But entries came from surprising sources including graduate students, consultants, mathematicians, and military officers, all seeking a piece of the action. "We had applied math, advanced physics, intelligent systems, computer graphics and organic solutions to inorganic problems. There were capabilities I had never seen before in the industry," says McEwan.

"When I saw the computer graphics I almost fell out of my chair." The contestants had identified 110 targets on the Red Lake property, 50 percent of which had not

been previously identified by the company. Over 80 percent of the new targets yielded substantial quantities of gold. In fact, since the challenge was initiated an astounding eight million ounces of gold have been found. McEwen estimates the collaborative process shaved two to three years off their exploration time.

Today Goldcorp is reaping the fruits of its open-source approach to exploration. Not only did the contest yield copious quantities of gold, it catapulted his underperforming $100 million company into a $9 billion juggernaut while transforming a backward mining site in northern Ontario into one of the most innovative and profitable properties in the industry. Needless to say McEwen is one happy camper. As are his shareholders. One hundred dollars invested in the company in 1993 is worth over $3,000 today.

Perhaps the most lasting legacy of the Goldcorp Challenge is the validation of an ingenious approach to exploration in what remains a conservative and highly secretive industry. Rob McEwen bucked an industry trend by sharing the company's proprietary data and simultaneously transformed a lumbering exploration process into a modern distributed gold discovery engine that harnessed some of the most talented minds in the field.

The Goldcorp story flies in the face of much conventional wisdom about how to run a business. Companies seek to protect their intellectual property, and through hiring and retaining the best people they generate new ideas, make new discoveries, compete, and grow their business lines. McEwen saw things differently. He realized the uniquely qualified minds to make new discoveries were probably outside the boundaries of his organization, and by sharing some intellectual property he could harness a powerful new force—mass collaboration. In doing so he stumbled successfully into the future of innovation, business, and how wealth and just about everything else will be created.

Due to deep changes in technology, demographics, business, the economy, and the world, we are entering a new age where people participate in the economy like never before. This new participation has reached a tipping point where new forms of mass collaboration are changing how goods and services are invented, produced, marketed, and distributed on a global basis. This change presents far-reaching opportunities for every company and for every person who gets connected."

If nothing else, this passage from *Wikinomics* is a perfect illustration of what Alvin and Heidi Toffler described in *Revolutionary Wealth*. Billions of connected individuals can now actively participate in innovation and wealth creation in ways we once only dreamed of. And when these masses of people collaborate they can collectively advance the arts, culture, science, education, government, and the economy in surprising but ultimately profitable ways. Companies that engage with these exploding Web-enabled communities are already discovering the true dividends of collective capability and genius.

One such company is Marshall-Wace Asset Management—one of GaveKal's three initial clients and a company on whose advisory board Charles sits. Five years ago, MWAM started work on a new application called TOPS whose core idea was initially very simple: at a time when everyone derided the sell-side research analysts and brokers as either a) a waste of time and money or worse yet b) intellectually dishonest market participants who were only to happy to sell out to the diktats of investment bankers (i.e.: the whole Henry Blodget, Jack Grubman etc… fiasco) Ian Wace, Paul Marshall, Anthony Clake and the other MWAM partners took the bet that there was a reason that the equity brokerage industry generates upward of US$50bn of commission a year. And this reason was that the armies of analysts and brokers that the sell-side employs could actually deliver a tremendous amount of added-value. The only problem, of course, was harnessing this "alpha" in a reliable and systematic way. And this is how TOPS was born.

TOPS is a web-based global platform that MWAM delivers to equity-brokers and equity research analysts in Europe, North America, Latin America, Japan and Asia. TOPS contributors have, at all times, a portfolio of equities to manage with the ability to either go long, or short any equities they please. MWAM then compiles this information and tries to filter out the most interesting data points. The TOPS system allows MWAM to quickly see:

- How a given piece of news (i.e.: earnings release, a new CEO...) is likely to be interpreted by the market

- A sudden change of mood by the sell-side on a given stock, or sector

- Who amongst brokers and analysts is consistently good - and who is consistently bad!

- How the overall market is positioned

- Opportunities that may be currently overlooked by the market (i.e.: if one can find a company with good earnings growth, solid pricing momentum and yet few analysts and brokers are bothering to recommend it, then the stock may have decent upside)

With its TOPS system, MWAM has effectively re-engineered the relation between the buy and sell side and transformed it into a mass-collaboration, horizontal network. This of course was only possible though large investments in technology; but with these investments made, MWAM can now claim to have created a new, dynamic, way of investing money which relies on peer production and collective knowledge rather than any one individual.

From gold mining to money management, it is not a stretch to say that our entire way of doing business is being re-organized in front of our very eyes and that we are still only just at the beginning of the "mass collaboration" revolutionary trend. And this trend should boost global growth for years to come.

Progress, R&D and Technology

We are usually loath to quote politicians, especially those on the Far Left, but this paragraph from Speaker of the House Nancy Pelosi's op-ed piece in the Wall Street Journal entitled "R&D Democrats" says it all: "America has always been committed to being number one. Every scientific advance once thought impossible that has been achieved–splitting the atom, landing a man on the moon, mapping the human genome–has been achieved by Americans. We accomplished these extraordinary goals, and then benefited from the jobs, industries and successive innovations they have yielded because our country was willing to make two critical commitments. We invested in the education and ambition of the American people, and we promoted an entrepreneurial culture that supports long term, high risk ideas."

And this is a great point. Where do some of the things we take for granted, the everyday items like Pyrex cookware, or velcro fasteners, or light-emitting diodes come from? All around us, from color laser printers to mass spectrometers, from the computer mouse to open-sided MRIs, from satellite radio to all-aluminum engines (which save weight and improve performance), from Teflon pans to "natural light" bulbs... we stand in awe of the products churned out by research and development efforts of companies around the world. Even the ability of our Captain Crunch cereal to stay crunchy for at least fifteen minutes is a testament to the research and development capabilities of General Mills!

BASF, the German chemical company, has a commercial that states "we don't make the things you buy, we make the things you buy better." Increasingly that is becoming more true of platform companies. In our book *Our Brave New World*, we described the three broad functions of companies: to design a product, to manufacture a product and to distribute a product. And successful companies in the Western world are deciding to focus their resources on the first—designing products.

In the forgone US manufacturing age, growth was achieved by physically producing, with company-owned assets, more of the same products. Improvements in quality, whether it be in size or speed or otherwise, was not of primary concern (anyone who owned an American-made car in the 1970s or 1980s can attest to that). Increases in volumes, without damaging pricing, were easily achievable with proper planning because there was not an abundance of supply relative to demand. With the Cold War, trade restrictions and misguided monetary policies, global markets were less efficient and price was easier to realize.

In the 1980s, with the backdrop of a falling rate of inflation and freer trade, vertically integrated companies realized they could enhance profitability by locating productive assets in places like Japan and Korea—they began the process of de-verticalization. This relocation of fixed assets drove profitability by allowing companies to shed capital consuming functions and focus on profit producing ones.

Then, in the early 1990s, the opportunity to outsource the manufacture of an entire product availed itself as global borders opened and capital flowed more freely around the world. Highly efficient producers that could fulfill any order with impressive quality and speed sprang up everywhere, from Southeast Asia to Korea, from Central America to Eastern Europe.

The technology revolution was an accelerant to this trend of outsourcing, as far flung participants in a supply chain could be connected and efforts coordinated. Just in time inventories, supply chain management and business process outsourcing become part of the lexicon of business.

Platform companies realized that in a deflationary boom environment, characterized by plentiful physical fulfillment, to sustain profits and to grow, they had little choice but design new features, improve existing products and create whole new products or product categories. In short, they had to become more productive. In a world characterized by ever faster creative destruction, companies that stand still are bound to end up as road kill.

Nevertheless, this meant a different kind of investment than in the past. Today, less capital is being invested in the expansion of physical capacity and more capital is being invested in the expansion of intellectual capacity. In the following pages, we look at a cross-section of some of America's largest companies. From technology to auto manufacturers, from drugs to aerospace… And everywhere we care to look, we note the following trends in R&D expenses relative to capital expenditures:

- They have grown much faster

- They were unaffected by recessions, mid-cycle slowdowns or financial crises

- The rate of increase, in some cases, is accelerating

- The trends really diverged in the early 1990s (the beginning of the explosion in the trade deficit)

- They have led to strong productivity gains

Reviewing these trends, we have a tough time getting too worried about the outlook for US equities, or for the US economy.

Let us start with an industry in which R&D is crucial: pharmaceuticals. Note the divergence in spending trends at Pfizer. In 1991, R&D, at $1 billion was only 25% bigger than Capex of $800 million. But after growing at a near +15% compound rate, R&D is now almost 3x the size of Capex.

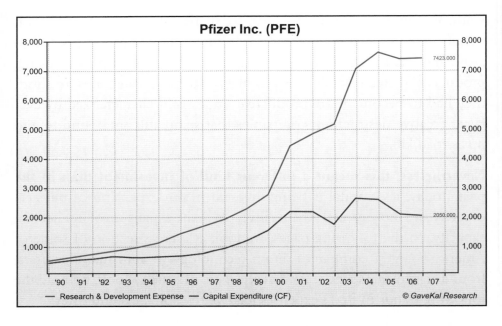

At Johnson and Johnson, the surge in R&D relative to Capex is more pronounced as the two costs began the 1990s at parity. But in the past 15 years, R&D has grown at a 12% compound rate while Capex has grown at a +6% rate. Now annual R&D expenses are 2.5x annual capital expenditures. Neither mid-cycle slowdown nor recession effected R&D, though it definitely affected Capex.

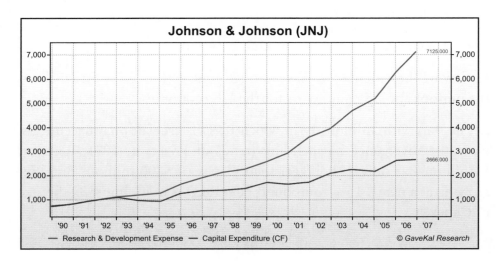

Moving on to technology, Microsoft has grown its R&D at +25% compounded over the last 15 years. The 1997 bulge was likely linked to the efforts to get Windows 98 out the door.

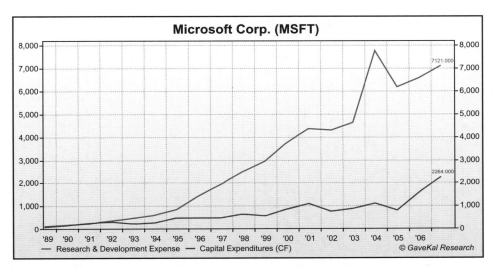

Microsoft Corp. (MSFT)

— Research & Development Expense — Capital Expenditures (CF)   © GaveKal Research

We witness a similar trends at Oracle, with R&D growing at +22%, while Capex has been in outright decline since 1996. Annual R&D expenses are almost now 10x the size of Capex.

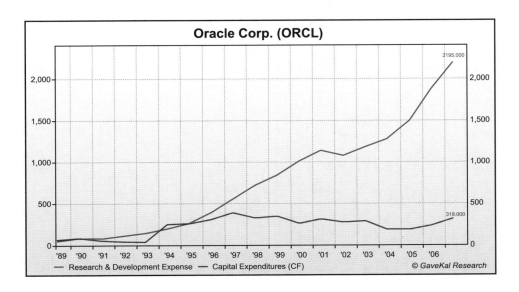

Oracle Corp. (ORCL)

— Research & Development Expense — Capital Expenditures (CF)   © GaveKal Research

And the same is true of industrial companies. Boeing's R&D doubled over the last decade and a half, while Capex has been halved. The acceleration in R&D from 2000 to present in the face of a recession and a stock market crash is rather impressive. Apparently, Dreamliner's are very expensive to design...

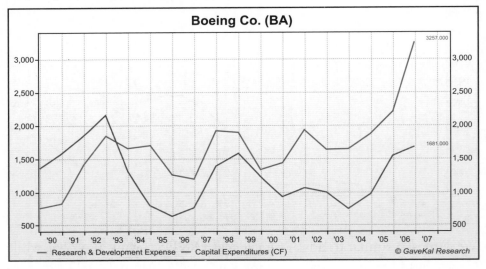

Boeing Co. (BA)

3257.000

1681.000

— Research & Development Expense — Capital Expenditures (CF)   © GaveKal Research

We witness a similar trend with United Technologies. Despite the fact that durable goods deflation has been highly pernicious in recent years, UTX still managed to turn in an all-time record operating margins last year!

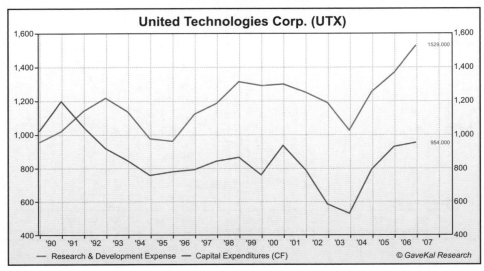

United Technologies Corp. (UTX)

1529.000

954.000

— Research & Development Expense — Capital Expenditures (CF)   © GaveKal Research

For the first time in its history, Dupont spent more on R&D in 2004 than it did on Capex. Notice Capex is a fifth the level it was in 1991.

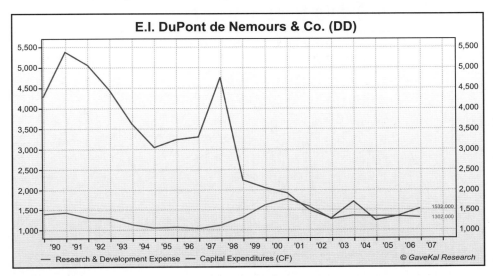

Should we be surprised by the fact that Ford spent more on R&D last year than on Capex? Almost $500m more! Capex has been flat for 15 years while R&D has doubled. Unfortunately, fuel cells, heads-up displays, satellite radios, hybrid engines, airbags, anti-lock brakes, drive-by-wire tech... don't invent themselves.

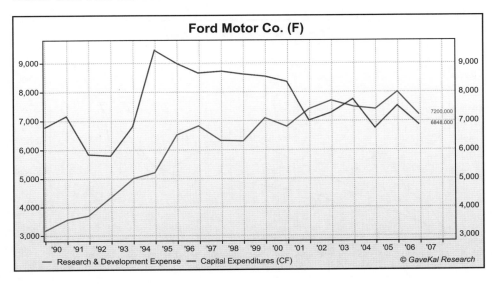

Another example of stagnant Capex and vibrant research and development can be found at Proctor and Gamble. In the next recession, Capex will likely fall to levels permanently lower than R&D.

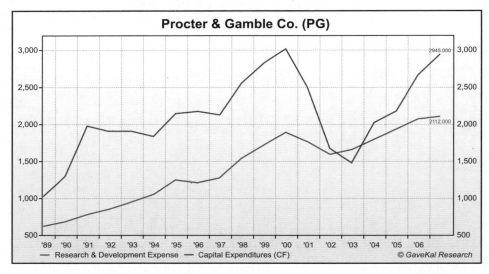

Procter & Gamble Co. (PG)

— Research & Development Expense — Capital Expenditures (CF)   © GaveKal Research

As an example of the productivity of the R&D investments, let's review sales per employee at P&G. They were roughly $275,000/employee in 1991. Today, they stand nearer to $525,000/employee—that represents a +4.5% annual growth.

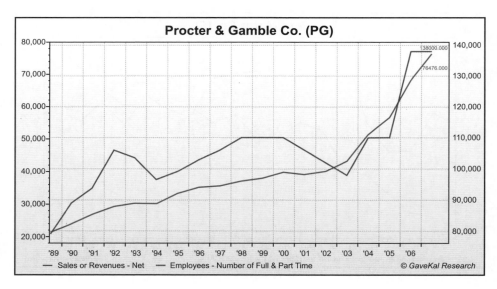

Procter & Gamble Co. (PG)

— Sales or Revenues - Net   — Employees - Number of Full & Part Time   © GaveKal Research

Putting it all together, we find it hard to understand the pessimists' mantra that the US economy is on the verge of implosion. Looking at capital spending numbers gives a very incomplete picture of the health, and innovation, prevalent across the US corporate sector. In *Our Brave New World*, what matters is R&D, not Capex. And those who do not keep in mind the R&D trends will continue to miss an important piece of the puzzle. But of course keeping tabs on the global Innovation Boom is no walk in the park!

The Need For New Accounting Rules

For years, measuring the investments made by companies and the returns generated by those investments was easy: all we had to do was look at a) the money a company allocated to capital spending and b) the returns on equity that the company generated as a function of those investments. The difference between Return on Capital and Cost of Capital—Economic Value Added—was like one stop shopping in assessing the efficiency with which a company was deploying capital.

Today, as companies exit capital intensive manufacturing processes and concentrate more on design and distribution functions, they invest less money in capital expenditures and more money in research and development. And, as companies go through this transformation, relying on GAAP-based accounting for information falls way short of painting an accurate picture.

Indeed, amongst the failings of GAAP-based accounting we find that:

1. Research and Development is treated as an intermediate expense and not an investment. For example, the salaries of scientists at Pfizer engaged in developing the next blockbuster drug are lumped in with wages of the workers in the production facility.

2. Because of this, companies that spend an increasing portion of their investment dollars on R&D are penalized since R&D investments reduce earnings without boosting the balance sheet.

3. The benefits that accrue to companies investing heavily in R&D show up in other places than just the income statement. For example, successful investments in distribution initiatives result in improved working capital trends—like lower inventory levels—that are not captured on the income statement.

4. Companies that invest heavily in R&D have no asset on their balance sheet to show for their deployment of capital, thus skewing the appearance of their capital structure. For example, the value of Dell's supply chain infrastructure doesn't show up on its balance sheet. Neither does the value of Amazon's search engine (doesn't it sometimes feel as if Amazon knows what you want for Christmas better than your friends and family?).

The first thing that strikes us is the bad deal that R&D spending gets. As things stand, an investment in a tangible asset (e.g.: a machine tool...) is counted as a productive asset for years. Meanwhile, in accounting terms, the in-house development of an online distribution network (e.g.: iTunes) loses the entirety of its value within a year. How does this make sense?

One explanation might be that quantifying R&D is very challenging. In a 2001 survey of fund managers, private-equity investors, venture-capitalists and bank analysts entitled *A Survey of Investor Attitudes on IP Protection,* 90% of respondents considered a company's intellectual property an important factor in their investment assessment. At the same time, 70% of respondents felt there didn't exist adequate tools to measure intellectual property and 56% even asserted IP couldn't be measured at all. So a large majority agrees that investment in intangible assets is very important, and that it is tough to quantify. But is this difficulty justification enough for treating R&D as spending instead of development?

Carol Corrado, Charles Hulten and Daniel Sichel of the National Bureau of Economic Research (the group charged with officially calling recessions) have produced a series of papers, the most recent of which is

Intangible Capital and Economic Growth to deal with this very issue. They write: _"Any use of resources that reduces current consumption in order to increase it in the future qualifies as an investment. This result argues for the symmetric treatment of all types of capital, so that, for example, spending on R&D and employee training should be placed on the same footing as spending on plant and equipment. Moreover, this symmetry principle requires that most business expenditures aimed at enhancing the value of a firm and improving its products, including human capital development as well as R&D, be accorded the same treatment as tangible capital."_

They go on to develop their argument with the following:

"The symmetry principle… establishes the theoretical equivalence of tangible and intangible capital… Indeed, some have argued—particularly in the accounting world—that several characteristics of intangibles disqualify them from being counted as capital; namely, the lack of verifiability for intangible assets that are not acquired through market transactions; the lack of visibility of intangible assets after their acquisition that complicates efforts to track past vintages; the non-rivalness of some intangible assets; and the lack of appropriability of the returns from some intangibles."

These objections make a lot of sense and bring us back to the point above on how most investors are happy to put their hands up when it comes time to "valuing intangibles". Having said that, let us take a look at these objections individually:

1. Lack of Verifiability: We find it a bit odd that, because of "lack of verifiability", intangibles are de facto classified as an intermediate input. Imagine that you are a big pharmaceutical company: if you develop a drug in-house, it is an intangible. But if you buy the drug from a biotech start-up, it is an asset? The real issue of whether intangibles should be classified as intermediates, or as capital, depends on the economic character of the good; not the ease with which it can be measured.

2. Lack of Visibility: There is no doubt that tangible goods have a physical embodiment that is capable of being observed. Touching the machine tools that produce the cars at Ford is easy to do. Meanwhile, intangibles have no palpable embodiment and definitely lack visibility (the old adage of how the bank's assets take the elevator everyday).

But this concern is not a valid conceptual reason for treating intangibles as an intermediate input rather than as a capital asset. Again, it is how the item is used over time that determines whether or not it should be capitalized.

3. Non-rivalness: As we mentioned in the previous chapter, in their book *Revolutionary Wealth*, Alvin and Heidi Toffler enumerate *"how profoundly different knowledge is from any other resource or assets that go into the creation of wealth. Knowledge is a) inherently non-rival, b) intangible, c) non-linear, d) relational, e) mates with other knowledge, f) is more portable than any other product, g) can be compressed into symbols or abstractions, h) can be stored in smaller and smaller spaces, i) can be explicit or implicit, expressed or not expressed, shared or tacit, and j) is hard to bottle up. Putting all these characteristics together, we wind up with something so unlike the tangibles with which economists have traditionally been concerned that many of them just shake their heads and, like most people, seek comfort in the world they know. The non-rivalness of pure knowledge implies that it can be employed by many users simultaneously without diminishing the quantity available to any single user."*

4. Non-appropriability: One of the major problems for accountants is that the full benefits of R&D and, even more so, of worker training may not be captured by the firm making the investment. It may instead be captured by the employees (e.g.: employees leave their investment banking jobs to set up highly successful hedge funds. Or marginally successful economic research firms...). Consequently, the measured prices may reflect only private benefits and cost, not true investments...

Nevertheless, these two features (non-rivalness and non-appropriability) do not invalidate the need to capitalize intangible expenditures. As Corrado, Hulten and Sichel explain: *"In sum, the various characteristics that cause tangible and intangible capital to be different -verifiability, visibility, non-rivalness, and appropriability- are all important features that distinguish one type of capital from the other. However, none of these differences is relevant to the issue of whether to treat intangible expenditures as capital. That is determined by whether or not the expenditure is intended to yield output in some future period."*

Estimates of the amount of money invested in intangible assets vary. The Corrado, Hulten and Sichel study estimates the figure at US$800 billion (based on 2003 data). Leonard Nakamura from the Federal Reserve Bank of Philadelphia puts the total at US$1 trillion in 2004. And Kevin Logan of DKW put the total at US$1.3 trillion for 2005. Note that all these numbers may be correct. After all, non-residential fixed investment (the National and Income Product Account that represents capital expenditures) totals just over US$1 trillion and, as we tried to show in the previous chapter, in a growing number of US companies, the amount spent on R&D is now far greater than the amount spent on fixed capital. **In any event, there is no doubt that the unrecognized impact of investment in intangible assets is large-and growing.**

Gary Bachula, the former US undersecretary of commerce, once said: *"Leading economists now identify technical progress as a major, if not the single most important factor in sustained economic growth, accounting for as much as one half of US economic growth in the past 50 years."* And in *Strategy in an Era of Global Giants: The World's Biggest Companies are Learning to Manage Complexity,* authors Lowell Bryan and Michel Zanini state: *"Today's most successful large companies have a more nuanced formula for success. They are exploiting their size and scope, as well as the large number of talented professionals they employ, to combine tangible and intangible assets across the enterprise. In this way, they create unique capabilities and value propositions that help them achieve a distinctive and durable competitive edge.... The evidence suggest that during the past decade, some mega-institutions developed strategies and organizational models, largely involving intangible assets, that help them to produce extraordinary profits and to exploit their economies of scale and scope more effectively."*

The evidence is inescapable: the global economy and business models are transforming, largely due to the employ of intangible assets. Despite the measurement difficulties, in a quantitative and qualitative sense, **the**

allocation of capital into intangible assets meets the test for investment. It is a use of a resource that reduces current consumption in order to increase it in the future.

This brings us back to another passage from the Tofflers' new book: *"In an economy based more and more on knowledge and innovation, this creates a challenging problem not just for economists but for economics… The rise of knowledge intensity is not just a minor bump in the road… We are, in fact living through the deepest upheaval in the world knowledge system since our species started to think. Until we digest this point, our best-laid plans for the future will misfire."*

In today's world, GAAP accounting methods are rapidly becoming obsolete. And this makes the job of professional investors increasingly challenging. In order to identify the companies that we want to invest in, we have spent a lot of time, and effort, rebuilding company accounts for US corporation which, we believe, reflect a more accurate picture than the one provided by GAAP. But let us be clear here: much greater minds than our own have been working on this for some time and have so far come up empty. However, having said that, we do benefit from one great advantage over academics and accountants: like Lord Keynes, we are perfectly content being approximately right rather than precisely wrong.

CHAPTER 20

Reasons For Optimism Beyond the Current Crunch

At this stage, it should be obvious to our reader that we firmly believe that George Soros' 60-year credit "super-cycle" has not been the only, nor in our view the most important, of the "super-booms" driving the world economy. Three other great secular trends have been even more powerful, namely:

- The arrival of 3 billion new workers and consumers in the world economy

- The global division of labour which results from almost universal free trade

- The reduction of transport, communication and data processing costs to virtually zero

These secular trends and their consequences are nowhere near exhausted even if it turns out that George Soros is right to argue that the credit super-cycle is now over.

George Soros assumes that any huge boom, like the ones seen in credit and consumption, must be followed by an equally huge bust, because markets never return to equilibrium–they always overshoot, both on the way up and the way down. **But this assumption, justified by Soros' focus on reflexivity, ignores another and even more powerful force in both economics and human nature: rationality.**

Businesses and workers driven by the profit motive have a natural bias to try to create wealth, rather than destroy it–and they elect governments to support, rather than sabotage, this process. Soros is right that markets are fallible and that they have a natural tendency to create reflexive boom-bust cycles. A world of pure market fundamentalism, with absolutely no regulation of market forces, would therefore degenerate into the mad-house of manic-depressive speculation Soros describes. This, however, is not the real world. Laissez-faire politicians constantly over rule market forces when they face serious economic crises. And politicians are naturally less eager to limit excessive booms than devastating busts.

There are, of course, times when governments make mistakes and fail to stimulate an economy enough to prevent a serious recession. There are also situations where governments and central banks are constrained in providing stimulus, either by high inflation or by international constraints, such as membership in the ERM or the Euro. In general, however, it is much more likely that politicians will err on the side of too much stimulus, rather than doing too little too late. This is the main reason why the world economy has a natural bias towards long booms and short, shallow slowdowns.

Our hunch is thus that a combination of monetary and fiscal easing along with some regulatory changes is now very likely as a pure market solution has failed. This should ease the credit crisis and prevent a world recession. But we may, of course, be wrong. At this stage, the main question for investors should be whether the destabilising reflexivity stressed by George Soros or the stabilising rationality in which we broadly believe will turn out to be the main force driving the world economy this year.

But having said, there are other policy changes that we need to consider in our investment roadmap. And these changes are taking place in Asia.

PART 2

The Change In Policy

The Long Shadow of the Asian Crisis

It is hard to underestimate the lingering impact the 1997-98 Asian Crisis had on Asian policymakers. In 1997, in the space of a few months, the near entire burgeoning middle-class of numerous countries was wiped out. And (more alarmingly for policymakers), following this disaster, few policymakers got to keep their jobs. In Indonesia, Suharto was toppled. In Malaysia, a power struggle landed the Deputy Prime Minister, Anwar Ibrahim, in jail for six years. In the Philippines, a wild-card former movie-star was elected to the presidency. In Thailand, a telecoms billionaire was elected Prime Minister (both would later be ousted unconstitutionally)…

With the Financial Crisis, Asian policy makers basically learnt one lesson: having an overvalued exchange rate, seeing central bank reserves shrink, running current account deficits, having the IMF in town… all these are things that must be avoided at all cost. And if the cost is to maintain an undervalued exchange rate, then so be it.

As it turns out, the foreign exchange markets have always been the place where the governments of the world have felt free to manipulate the markets, without restraint. From fixed exchange rate systems, to dirty floats, to exchange rates manipulated for mercantilist or political reasons, the list is long and the stories seldom end happily (Argentina in 2001, Asia in 1997, UK in 1992…). Still, for the past decade, Asian central banks have by and large felt that maintaining an artificially low exchange rate was the path to prosperity.

And to be fair, for the past decade, this has led to some prosperity for Asia. After all, the sustained undervaluation of any currency typically allows for an abnormally high rate of return on invested capital in the "goods-producing" part of the economy (think how well Toyota does, and how poorly Ford does, when the Yen is weak and the US$ is high). An undervalued currency can thus be viewed as a subsidy to local production. And, more often than not, this subsidy is paid by the local consumer (who can afford to buy less foreign made goods). A sustained undervaluation also leads to massive FDI (foreign direct investments) inflows and, typically, to trade surpluses. In the other countries, an undervalued currency can be viewed as a subsidy to consumption (in our example above, thanks to a cheaper Yen, Americans can buy more Toyotas…); this subsidy is paid for by local producers (i.e.: Ford).

So today, if we are right in our assertion that Asian currencies have been manipulated downwards so as to remain undervalued, then we can say that:

- Production in Asia has being subsidized to the detriment of Asian consumption

- Consumption outside of Asia (especially in the US and Europe) has been subsidized to the detriment of ex-Asian production

To a large extent, this big subsidy to consumption has been visible for all to see in the US. Who, by now, has not heard of the over-extended, over-weight, over-leveraged, glutonous American consumer? But the subsidy seems to have had far less of an impact on the other major global economic sphere, Europe. Or has it?

Indeed, as Bastiat once said, in economics, there is always "what you see, and what you don't see". What everyone sees is the "prodigality" of the US consumer. What few see is that this attitude to spend come hell or high-water is matched across the pond not by the European consumer, but instead by European governments.

Indeed, we would go as far as saying that the structure of consumption is markedly different between the US and Europe. It would be our guess (though note that this is just a guess) that, in the US, 75% of what is described as "consumption" is done directly by the private sector while 25% is done by public entities (government spending, social security etc...). Meanwhile, in most European countries, the ratio is probably closer to 50-50.

Why does this distinction matter? Because the two sets of players react to very different factors. The private sector tends to react to prices (i.e.: flat screens TVs get so cheap that everyone buys one), while the public sector tends to react to the ability to borrow without having an undue impact on interest rates. In other words, as long as a politician can borrow and spend, the chances are that he will (witness George W. Bush's impressive expansion in the federal government in his first term).

Moreover, since the competition coming from an undervalued currency impacts only the private sector, the effects on the two groups will be widely divergent.

Subsidizing Consumption in the US:

When the Asian central banks maintain artificially low exchange rates against the US$, the production of goods in which the US does not have a solid comparative advantage (i.e.: cars?) does not stand a chance. In such goods, we have a structural decline in prices, not always compensated by a rise in volumes.

The decline in the price of such goods leads to a massive increase in the standard of living of most consumers and a rise in real disposable income. This excess disposable income then triggers real estate price increases and increases in service prices (more on that later). It also accelerates the transformation of US companies into platform companies. And, in turn, this has two consequences: an impressive increase in corporate earnings and a simultaneous deterioration in the US trade balance. The two are like two sides of the same coin since, by adopting the platform company model, US corporations are in essence saying "you can take the jobs and the sales; we will take the profits" and, of course, the current account deficit is measured on sales, not profits (more on that later)!

Strong corporate earnings, rising housing and booming domestic consumption then lead to a massive increase in tax receipts. This, in turn, means that, despite George W. Bush's great expansion in federal spending (the largest single expansion since Johnson's "Great Society"), the US budget deficit stand today at below 2% of GDP. As a result, gross US government debt as a percentage of GDP has remained fairly stable (in the 60%-70% range) since 1990:

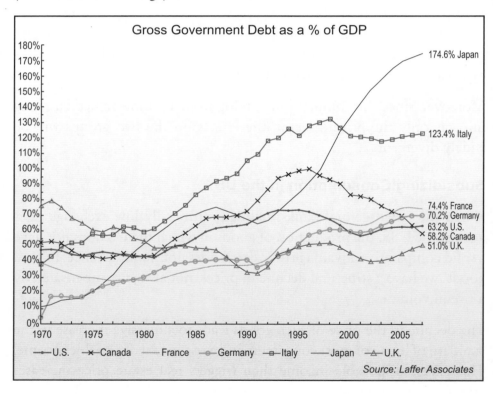

The same, of course, cannot be said of Europe where government debt has undeniably been on the increase. In both France and Germany, gross government debt as a percentage of GDP has, since 1990, made a serious jump higher (from the 35%-40% range to the 70%-75% range).

Subsidizing Consumption in Europe:

Milton Friedman famously said that there were four kinds of money: (1) the kind of money that you earn yourself and spend on yourself–this kind, you tend to be very careful with; (2) the kind of money that you earn yourself and spend on someone else–this kind you tend to be a little less careful with; (3) the kind somebody else earns and you spend–which is easy to go a little wild with; and finally (4) there is the kind of money that you do not earn and that is spent on somebody else–this money, Milton Friedman showed, is never wisely spent!

In the US, the subsidy provided by the Asian government to consumption has been cashed in by the consumer. It has thus been the first kind of "Milton Friedman money". In Europe, the subsidy provided by the Asian currency manipulation has instead, and as the above chart illustrates, been rapaciously grabbed by governments. It has been the fourth kind of "Milton Friedman money".

Why do governments not spend as wisely as consumers? For a start, the propensity of a public consumer to import is much lower than the propensity of an individual consumer to import (i.e.: public officials would rather use money to buy votes than get the best price for a good or a service). In turn, this leads to a much lower trade deficit, but also a much lower increase in the standard of living (i.e.: David Ricardo's law of comparative advantages isn't allowed to unleash its full benefits). In turn, this leads to less growth, which then leads to less consumption, itself leading to fewer imports...

If the US consumer was using the Asian subsidy to buy himself a new flat screen TV or a third car, what were the European governments doing with their subsidy? On what did they spend the 30-40% of GDP deterioration in gross government debt? It is of course hard to pin the losses on any one factor. Needless to say, subsidizing a train system which each year loses the equivalent of half of the national education budget (as the SNCF in France regularly does) doesn't help. Neither does the maintenance of expensive social safety nets at times when the unemployment rate seems to remain stubbornly stuck in double-digit territory (Germany, France, Italy…). But whatever the culprit is, the result is the same: a very limited growth rate and a constant deterioration of the budget deficits.

This is what has been happening for the past ten years. But will it continue to be the case for the next ten years? We do not think so.

The Circle of Manipulation Comes to An End

The Asian central banks' unwavering desire to maintain undervalued exchange rates has had massive ripple effects throughout the economy. In 2004, we started referring to this pattern as "The Circle of Manipulation" and we believe that the so-called circle looked a little like this:

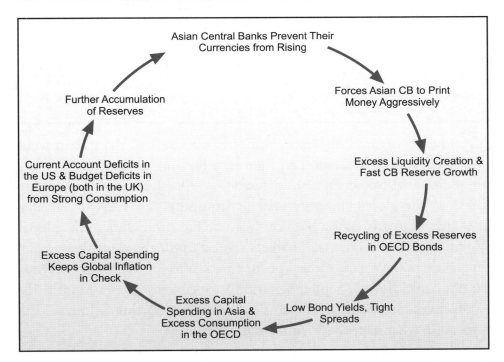

In 2003 and 2004, the circle was given a further boost by the fact that OECD central banks, worried about a massive Japanese-style deflationary bust, pushed large amounts of liquidity into the system. The Tech bust, the Enron scandal and the 9/11 terrorist attacks all encouraged more liquidity creation, which in turn fuelled various bubbles around the world:

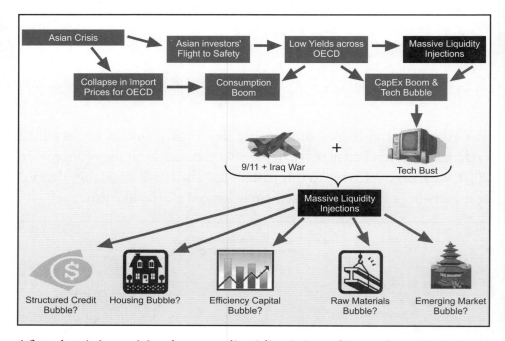

After the Asian crisis, the extra liquidity injected into the system went into the technology sector, and then into housing (which, at the time, offered strong fundamentals). In the late 1990s, these were the "strong links" in the global financial system. Ironically, ten years to the day after the Asian crisis, Asia has now become the strong link in the global system and, as the financial markets started to hit the skids this spring, this is where the excess money pushed back into the system by nervous central banks flowed. September and October were banner months for Asian investors. Then, in November, the wheels starting falling off the wagon. So what happened? And what happens next?

In recent years, investors have basically had the choice to invest in one of three main asset "baskets".

- The first basket was the "winners of the current cycle". This basket includes Brazil, Russia, India, China, the Middle-East, Australia, Energy, Soft Commodities, Gold and other Precious Metals, Steel, Heavy Machinery, Infrastructure Spending, etc... This basket had, until recently, the strongest momentum but unfortunately also sported the highest valuations. To a large extent, this is the basket that is the most likely to evolve into a true bubble. And more than any other, this basket has been the prime beneficiary of the "Circle of Manipulation" described above.

- The second basket was the "losers of the current cycle". This basket includes OECD real estate, financials all over the world, US & EMU consumer spending and, we believe, EMU government spending. This basket has taken the brunt of the current correction and despite the large price-drops, it is very hard to tell whether this basket is now "undervalued" or not since a) no-one has a clue as to the standing of the balance sheets of the underlying companies and b) there is no visibility whatsoever as to the future profits (or losses) that this basket will generate.

- The third basket was "the bubbles of previous eras". Indeed, as most of us are painfully aware, once a bubble bursts, it usually takes years, if not decades, before assets that were in a bubble regain their bubble high prices. More often than not, once a bubble bursts, asset prices tend to languish, unloved by investors. We threw in this basket Japan, Thailand, Malaysia, Taiwan, Technology, US Large-Cap Growth Stocks, etc... We have argued that this basket today groups some of the most undervalued assets in the world though, unfortunately they are undervalued for a reason: very little earnings growth in the pipeline.

Over the past few months, investors have thus had the choice to buy expensive assets and hope that growth and momentum continue, beaten-up assets with limited visibility, or cheap assets with tame growth. And of course, the winning portfolios in 2007 massively over-weighted basket

#1, shorted basket #2 aggressively, and largely ignored basket #3. But will this still be the winning portfolio strategy in 2008?

In our August 2008 piece _Why We Remain Bullish on Asian Equities_ we argued that investors needed to remain focused on basket #1. And our argument was simple: as basket #2 imploded, OECD central banks would flush the system with money. However, money never flows back into the "burst bubbles" and instead always flows to the "strong links". This time around, the "strong link" was obviously basket #1, and so it seemed logical that the excess liquidity pushed out by OECD central banks would make its way to the Asian equity markets and the various instruments used by investors to participate in Asia's growth (commodities, steel, infrastructure spending plays etc...). And, for a while, this worked like a charm... But then something changed.

That something was, of course, the willingness of Asian central banks to sit back and see prices in basket #1 rise continuously. Indeed, imagine for a second being in the shoes of Zhou Xiaochuan, the governor of the PBoC. This is what, until recently, you had to confront: a) a roaring bull market in real estate, b) a raging bubble in equities, c) rapidly rising food prices, d) soaring energy costs and, e) putting all of the above together, an inflation rate of 7%+, i.e.: much above one's comfort zone.

Of course Mr. Zhou was not the only one; all over Asia, central bankers were being re-acquainted with Milton Friedman's rule that a central bank can control its money supply growth rate/inflation rate, its exchange rate, and its interest rate... but cannot control all three simultaneously. And the central bankers were reminded of the rule the hard way: by a break-out in domestic inflation. And inflation forced Asian countries to reconsider their policies of FX manipulations.

As we write, we are now confronting an investment environment whereby most of "basket 2" is imploding before our very eyes. Watching the devastation unleashed in their financial sectors, the central banks of the OECD feel compelled to act and are thus either flooding the system with liquidity (ECB) or cutting interest rates aggressively (Fed). But of course, the extra money pushed into the system is not returning into "basket 2". Instead, it has mostly flowed into "basket 1".

Now in the bygone days of "The Circle of Manipulation", the excess liquidity flows coming out of the OECD would have been matched by liquidity creation in Asia which in turn would have triggered higher asset prices, more capital spending etc… But the big change, this time around, is that Asian policy-makers are allowing their currencies to rise. And in so doing, of course, they remove the subsidy to Western consumption which they have been providing for the past decade, hence "kicking" basket #2 while it is down.

And it is not just Asia that is having a problem with creeping prices. In fact, all across the Middle-East, rapidly rising prices are putting into serious question the existence of decade-old pegs.

In order for a currency peg to be successful, two economies linked by a common currency must be broadly aligned. For years, this is broadly what happened between the Gulf Cooperation Council (GCC) states and the United States. When the United States boomed, oil prices tended to rise (along with interest rates), and GCC countries boomed as well. Then, when the higher oil and higher interest rates weighed down the US economy, oil prices would start easing, thereby ensuring that GCC economies slowed somewhat as well. But lately, this relationship has completely broken down, with US growth slowing, US interest rates moving lower, oil making new highs and GCC economies going on a tear (the combination of high oil and low interest rates is especially potent for GCC countries).

As inflation accelerates across the Middle East, central bankers across the region are grappling (just like their counterparts in Asia) with Milton Friedman's golden rule. So should we expect the GCC central banks to break their pegs to the US$? Is it in their interest to do so?

In discussions with policymakers around the region, we have regularly been told that the pegs, the fall in the US$, and the consequent rise in import prices are not to blame for the rise in inflation. Instead, the main culprit is the rapid rise in property prices. For example, in the UAE, rents have increased by 50% in the past five years—and probably much more at the high-end, as the current expansion attracts more and more foreign workers. We are also told that, with a very large number of real estate developments due for completion from now until 2009, a good portion of the inflationary pressures should abate. Therefore, inflation, we are told, is not imported but homegrown. Meanwhile, as the IMF and ratings agencies argue, the peg offers stability to investors and importers....

There are, we believe, several fallacies to this line of argument:

- Firstly, property prices have to be somewhat a function of input costs in new developments. Steel, windows, fascia, copper, cement—as well as engineers and other professions—are all being bid up around the world, not least in the Middle East. And the weak domestic currencies do not help defray any of the construction costs.

- Secondly, while the rising rents may be linked to a growing influx of foreign workers, rents are by and large non-discriminatory (as we found out at our expense when we opened an office in Abu Dhabi last year.). So the rising rents are also impacting the local community. Moreover, combine the rising rents with the rapidly rising food prices, and it is difficult to argue that the GCC's rising prices are not having a social impact.

- Thirdly, by ignoring the social costs of inflation, one inherently assumes that there will be an endless supply of workers at a fixed price. While this may be true for house services (barely), it is clearly no longer the case for mid-level professions. Indeed, besides competitive demands from the rest of the world, the old fertile labor supply countries (India, Philippines, Indonesia…) are themselves experiencing tremendous growth in their own right. And between working abroad without a family in a land where living costs are increasingly unaffordable, or staying at home for a less well-paid job, the decision is no longer an obvious one.

- Ignoring certain factor costs (the West ignores food and energy, the Middle East ignores housing…) is only sound if price spikes turn out to be temporary. But what happens if higher energy/food prices and/or housing prices turn out to be less cyclical or temporary?

- If, as Milton Friedman argued, inflation is always and everywhere a monetary phenomenon, then the argument that the pegs do not impact inflation is spurious, since the pegs contribute to rapid money supply growth (which then translates itself into higher real estate prices…).

- Lastly, and contrary to what the IMF may state, there is absolutely no evidence that the pegs have provided any stability to investors. Indeed, the costs for most infrastructure projects around the region are now being revised upwards by up to +50%. In fact, some energy infrastructure project costs have risen so much in the past year that they are being reviewed or abandoned altogether (for example, Exxon is now pulling out of developing an LNG/LPG refinery in Qatar).

Undeniably, inflation in the GCC countries is creeping higher. And it is hard to avoid the conclusion that the US$ pegs are the source of this problem. Inflation in the GCC is not simply a "homegrown" problem, but is increasingly related to imported cost-push inflation, itself a result of the weak US$ and the currency pegs. While demand-pull inflation is certainly one of the characteristics of fast-growing economies (especially in the housing space), there is little evidence that the GCC's inflation is purely domestic, or likely to abate any time soon. Ultimately, with negative real rates, exploding money growth and interest rates in the US likely to stay low for the foreseeable future, inflation, and especially asset price inflation, across the GCC countries is likely to stay too high for comfort. With the US currently entering into a mid-cycle slowdown with lower inflation and credit contraction, the GCC are on the opposite end of the spectrum: massive expansion. The current impact of pegged currencies means that local interest rates are no longer able to control local inflationary pressures.

Acknowledging this reality, Kuwait abandoned its peg in May and adopted a "basket of currencies" approach similar to Singapore's. Of course, it is a bit early to draw conclusions from this experience; but thus far, inflation remains high, though it does appear to be rolling over. We would not be surprised if, over the next 12 months, more Gulf states follow Kuwait's lead.

The global liquidity environment is thus changing before our very eyes. For a start, the US consumer is no longer pushing large amounts of money abroad through an ever-growing US current account deficit. For seconds, Asian & Middle-Eastern central banks are no longer as happy liquefying this current account deficit, accumulating reserves while their money supplies go through the roof. "The Circle of Manipulation" is well and duly broken. And with that, should we expect the portfolios that have delivered great returns for the past few years to continue doing so without a change? Probably not.

The Divergence in European Spreads–Why Now?

Back in May 2007, we wrote a piece entitled *"Part 2–So What Should We Worry About"*. In that ad hoc comment, we wrote: *"The crux of the thesis of our latest book, The End is Not Nigh, is simple and goes something like this: a) Asian central banks continue to manipulate their currencies and prevent them from finding a fair value against either the US$ or the Euro; b) this manipulation triggers an accumulation in central bank reserves which, in turn, leads to low real rates around the world; c) the combination of low global real rates and low Asian exchange rates amounts to a subsidy for Asian production and Western consumption; d) in the US, the subsidy has by and large been captured by individual consumers; e) meanwhile, in Europe, the subsidy has been cashed in by governments whose debt has skyrocketed; f) we see little reason why, in the near future, the subsidy should be removed; but g) if it were removed, the US would most likely encounter a consumer recession (not the end of the world); while h) Europe could go through a debt crisis (far more problematic)."*

We went on and wrote: *"Last week, and against most observers' expectations, the Indian central bank did not raise rates at its meeting. Instead, it seems that the authorities are allowing the currency to rise and hopefully thereby absorb some of the country's inflationary pressures (linked to energy and higher food prices). In recent weeks, the rupee has shot higher and now stands at a post-Asian crisis high. And interestingly, the local market is loving it. While Indian stocks had been sucking wind year to date, the central bank's apparent policy shift (from higher interest rates to higher exchange rates) has triggered a very sharp rally.*

This of course is an interesting turn of events and we would not be surprised if Asian central banks were to study developments in India carefully over the coming quarters. After all, India is blazing a path that a number of Asian countries may yet decide to follow.

One could argue that a change in monetary policy in Asia could end up being a "triple whammy" for Western economies. It would mean that:

- *Asian central banks would export less capital into our bond markets and this would likely lead to a drift higher in real rates around the world.*

- *Asian exchange rates would move sharply higher, which in turn would likely mean higher import prices in the US and Europe.*

- *As Asian exchange rates started to move higher, Asia's private savers would likely start repatriating capital, further amplifying exchange rate and interest rate movements. This would also likely lead to collapses in monetary aggregates in the Europe and the US.*

Finally, we concluded the paper by saying: *As we highlighted in Part 1: Why We Remain Bullish, we are not worried about valuations. And we are also not worried about "excess leverage" in the system, or the threat of a "private equity bubble". We also do not fear an "economic meltdown" or a brutal end to the "Yen carry-trade" (which we did fear in the Spring of 2006). Instead, if we had to have one concern, it would have to be a possible change of monetary policy across Asia and the impact that this would have on real rates around the world. As we view things, the only reason Asian central banks would change their policies is if food prices continued to increase (in that respect, owning some soft commodities—a hedge against rising real rates—makes sense to us; as does owning Asian currencies). Interestingly, such a turn of events seems to be unfolding in India, yet no one seems to care. Monitoring changes in Asian inflation, monetary policies and exchange rates could prove more important than ever.*

Nine months after that paper, we have indeed just gone through a period of a) rapidly rising food prices which have led to b) faster inflation rates across Asia, which have triggered c) a change in Asian monetary policy, notably a willingness to let the currencies appreciate faster than they have in the past. And if Asian central banks are now finally allowing their currencies to rise, then one thing is sure: Asian central banks will no longer need to print large amounts of their own currencies and accumulate US$ and Euros. They will thus also no longer need to buy UST and European bonds to the extent that they have.

Is it a coincidence that, as Asia starts to allow its currencies to rise, US mortgages have been hitting the wall and spreads amongst European sovereigns have started to widen? The subsidy that Asian central banks have been giving to consumption in the US and governments in Europe (see *The End is Not Nigh*) is now disappearing.

Indeed, for the past five years, spreads of Italian ten-year government bonds to German bonds have hovered between 15bp and 25bp. But recently, spreads have started to break out on the upside.

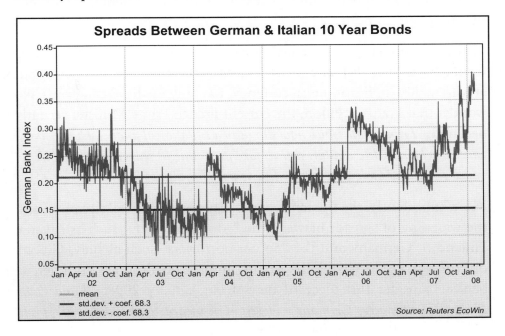

And, of course, Italy is not alone. All across Europe, we have seen a widening of spreads between the "stronger" signatures (Germany, Holland, Austria, Finland, Ireland) and the "weaker" signatures (Portugal, Italy, Greece, Spain, Belgium, France) including those of Eastern Europe (Latvia, Romania, Hungary, Poland…).

Now as our more seasoned GaveKal reader will undeniably remember (see *The End is Not Nigh*), we have argued that spreads between Europe's sovereigns were set to widen for the past few years. And yet, nothing happened. Until, that is, we started to see Asian central banks allowing their currencies to start appreciating faster.

So what happens if Asian central banks now stop buying up European government debt to the tune of recent years? For a start, European money supply growth should decelerate rapidly and with it, economic activity. A bigger problem will then be the ability of European governments to raise further financing. Indeed, as economic activity tanks in Europe, and the Euro starts to fall, it is likely that investors will all of a sudden realize that governments only go bust when they issue debt in a currency that they cannot print.

In the past fifteen years, France's government debt to GDP has moved from 35% in French Franc (i.e.: a currency the government could print at will) to 70% in Euros (i.e.: a currency that only the ECB can print). No wonder that Francois Fillon, the current French Prime Minister recently declared: *"I run a state which now stands in a situation of financial bankruptcy, which has known deteriorating deficits for fifteen straight years and which has not voted a balanced budget for twenty-five years. This cannot last."*

More importantly, the tightening-up of Europe's financial situation, and the widening of spreads between the "good borrowers" such as Austria, Finland or Germany and the "poorer borrowers" such as Italy, Greece, or Portugal, could have a devastating impact on Europe's commercial banks. Consider this piece of news from January 2008: *"Landesbank Baden-Wuerttemberg, Germany's biggest state-owned bank, said 2007 profit will be about 300 million euros ($438.9 million) because of a drop in prices of banking and government securities. LBBW said it doesn't expect any defaults since the securities concerned have good ratings."*

Less profits because of a drop in government securities? The careful reader may be somewhat surprised by this statement; after all, everywhere one cares to look across the OECD, government bond yields are close to their 2003 lows. So how did Germany's biggest state-owned bank manage to lose money on government securities? The answer, we believe, finds its source in the funky regulations of Basel II. According to Basel II, an OECD country bank can sell a credit default swap on an OECD sovereign and this CDS:

- Does not have to be marked to market (since it is assumed that an OECD country will not default on its debt).

- Does not require the selling bank to put aside any capital on its balance sheet (since, once again, it is assumed that the country on which the CDS is written will not default).

In other words, for the past few years, clerks all over Europe's banks and insurance companies have boosted the bottom line with the "free money" that the sale of CDS provided. Every now and then, a clerk at the Treasury department of ABC Landesbanken would call up Goldman Sachs or Deutsche Bank and say: "I want to sell US$1bn of protection on Italy at 15bp for five years". And for five years, ABC Landesbanken would receive US$1.5 million without having to set aside capital on its balance sheet or take a "mark to market" risk on its income statement. Or so it thought…

Indeed, as the spreads between Italy and Germany start to widen something unexpected happens *(a CDS will tend to reflect the spread between the issuer's debt and risk free debt of the same maturity. Otherwise an arbitrage could be made. If Italy's debt traded at 100bp over Germany and a CDS on Italy only cost 20bp, one could buy the Italian bond and buy the CDS and capture a "free" 80bp):* ABC Landesbanken receives a margin call from Goldman Sachs and Deutsche Bank and, all of a sudden, what was a "risk and capital free" trade turns out to impact the balance sheet. Needless to say, this is the situation we are now in and this probably contributes further to the widening of spreads. All of a sudden, Europe's commercial banks are no longer keen to sell the spread as they have been for the past decade… in fact, they are most likely trying to buy back some of the contracts they wrote before those move too far against them.

A widening of spreads represents the worst of both worlds for European banks. For a start, it puts their balance sheets under pressure. For seconds, it cuts down their income as the writing of CDS on Europe's weaker sovereigns slows to a crawl.

For Europe's policy-makers, the widening of spreads poses a serious challenge which, if left unchecked, could cut to the very credibility of the Euro and the European construction exercise. It could also trigger a negative spiral such as the one we saw in the US whereby as the cost of borrowing increases on the weakest signatures, rolling over debt becomes more problematic, hereby inviting higher spreads etc... So how will Europe's politicians respond to this new challenge?

The widening of credit spreads across Europe reflects an economic reality. It makes no sense that, say, Belgium and Ireland should borrow at the same rate.

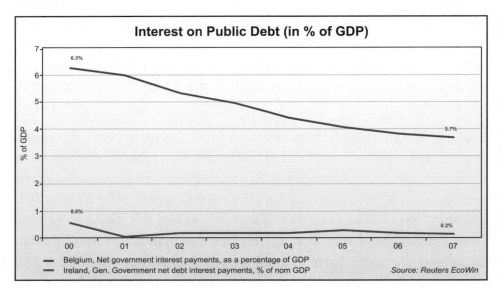

Interest on Public Debt (in % of GDP)

Belgium, Net government interest payments, as a percentage of GDP
Ireland, Gen. Government net debt interest payments, % of nom GDP

Source: Reuters EcoWin

The Euro 100bn question for investors should thus now be whether a) the recent widening is a one-off event and spreads are set to soon tighten again or b) the recent widening is the beginning of a more fundamentally-based re-pricing of risk across Euroland. The quandary now is whether politics can get us out!

In the mid 1990s, Europe's leaders got together and, in essence, said: "wouldn't it be great if we all got to borrow at the same rate as Germany?". And everyone around the table agreed that this would be a good thing. The decision was thus taken to a) create a currency which would resemble the DM, b) that this currency would be managed by a central bank with a mandate very similar to the Bundesbank's and c) that countries around the Euroland would strive to harmonize their fiscal policies (Maastricht Treaty rules and Stability and Growth Pact) to ensure the long-term survival of the Euro. At the time it was also envisaged that the collapse in interest rates in certain countries (Italy, Belgium, Spain...) would give a tailwind to growth which would allow governments around the more indebted EMU countries to tighten their belts and clean up their fiscal houses.

The collapse in interest rates happened, as yields converged to the German rate... but unfortunately, the clean-up in fiscal houses did not. In fact some countries like France cashed in the "growth dividend" and voted themselves greater benefits such as the 35-hour work week.

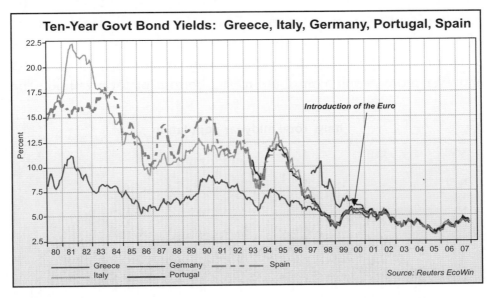

Which brings us to today and the recent widening of spreads across Europe. This widening is a sign that the market is starting to acknowledge that the promises have not been kept. **Thus, the best thing for Europe's governments would be to start keeping the promises that were made ten years ago.** But of course, the main problem with that solution is that it implies that Europe's governments will have to tighten their belts over the coming quarters, i.e.: at the worst possible time in the cycle. After all, it is always hard for a government to pull back and shrink its piece of the GDP cake… but in an economic slowdown, it is close to impossible.

It is all the harder to do when there is little political will for far-reaching reforms. As a former German central banker once told us: "I use to think that France needed a Margaret Thatcher, I now realize she needs an Arthur Scargill" (*Scargill was the Trotskyite leader of the Miner's Strike*). In other words, to get a government to shrink its size, you first need a serious crisis (or a scarecrow á la Scargill); only then do people accept real sacrifices.

And we should make no mistake about it: reforming Europe's welfare states will take real sacrifices. Take pensions as an example: for years, most European countries have run a pay-as-you-go system whereby people of my generation will pay directly for the retirement benefits of my dad's generation. In other words, Europe's pension systems are usually massive pyramid schemes; they work as long as the base grows and ever more people contribute to the bottom of the pyramid. The

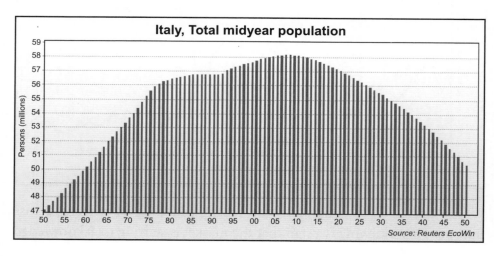

problem, of course, is that in a growing number of European countries, the base is no longer growing.

As such, the off-balance sheet liabilities assumed by the government in matters of pensions which, until recently, had always been self-funding, are now set to come back on the governments' balance sheets. Now the last time Europe ran a comprehensive survey of pension liabilities was in 2003... and the data back then was scary. We guess the situation does not look any better today.

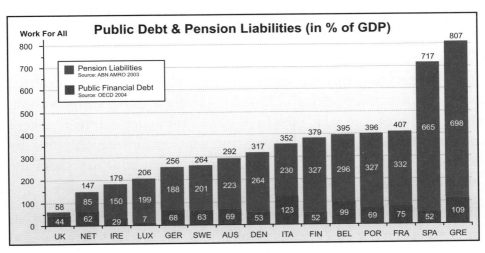

The deteriorating demographic and pension situation alone means that Europe's governments do need to contemplate serious pension reform. Or, failing that, to open their borders to workers from all horizons in order to keep expanding the tax-paying, pension-contributing workforce. Needless to say, neither of these options is very enticing politically. As such, rather than convince millions of pensioners to cut their benefits, or work longer, Europe's politicians may be tempted to try and convince a small minority of central bankers sitting in Frankfurt to massively ease monetary policy and print a bunch of money to help the governments meet their liabilities.

In essence, the scenario we are painting is a simple one: the credit crunch which has thus far mostly only engulfed the US is starting to make its way into Europe. And soon enough, Europe's banks will likely be reporting losses and write-downs, and investors will flee to the safety of the highest government bond paper. Unfortunately for Italy, Greece, Belgium or Portugal, their paper does not qualify as "high quality".

Now as we highlighted earlier in this book, a credit crunch typically invites a "three-step" policy response. First, one collapses the currency (to make one's assets and goods more attractive to foreign capital and invite inward capital flows). Secondly, one needs to see the banks recapitalized (if the market cannot do it, then the banks need to be nationalized). Thirdly, one puts in place a very steep yield curve in order to force the banks to start lending again and the private sector to take risk.

It is obvious today that this course of action is very much the preferred path of, for example, Nicolas Sarkozy. Hardly a day goes by without the French president taking the ECB to task for doing so little to relieve Europe's liquidity crunch. But his comments are increasingly met by rejoinders from Angela Merkel, the German Chancellor for whom the independence of the ECB is sacrosanct.

The possibility of a massive easing from the ECB is nonetheless an interesting one and raises the question of how the market will respond to a more activist ECB. Would an ECB that did the bidding of politicians be seen as less of a Bundesbank and more of a Bank of Italy/Banque de France? And if so, would long bond yields across Europe be below 4% and the Euro at 1.57/US$? Would the foreign central banks that have been piling into European government paper remain keen to finance Europe's welfare states?

Another question, of course, is what would happen in the event of a bank bankruptcy in Europe? Would the ECB bail out the failing bank? Would the government of a failing bank be allowed to bend the EU's competition rules and nationalize the troubled financial institution? These are all questions with answers that remain unclear.

Of course, there is another way to go about dealing with a credit crunch: bitter infighting. This is what Japan did throughout the 1990s when the MoF would tell the BoJ that massive monetary easing was needed, only for the BoJ to turn around and say that the MoF needed to stop financing the construction of bridges that went from nowhere to nowhere. And as the infighting ensued, the Japanese banking system wrote off its entire capital base not once, but twice, over the course of the decade. Meanwhile investors shied away from all asset classes save the highest quality government bonds.

Could the same thing unfold in Europe? In Japan, there were only three sets of players (the BoJ, the MoF and the LDP) and over fifteen years, they could not seem to get the three-step plan (currency devaluation, bank recap, steep yield curve) right. In that regard, when considering the numbers of players involved in Europe, one may fear that the same policy paralysis could easily grip Europe. And, in this case, the recent break-out in the spreads that has now started will prove to have marked the start of a revolutionary trend for our financial markets: the end of the convergence trades and the start of the divergence trades.

A few years before his death, Professor Milton Friedman declared: *"It seems to me that Europe, especially with the addition of more countries, is becoming ever-more susceptible to any asymmetric shock. Sooner or later, when the global economy hits a real bump, Europe's internal contradictions will tear it apart."* Today, one should question whether the "real bump" is being hit and whether Milton Friedman will end up being proven right. But regardless of where one falls on the answers to these questions, one thing is sure: selling the bonds of Europe's weakest signatures and buying protection on Europe's weaker banks continues to make sense. It is some of the cheapest protection available against what remains a massive "fat-tail" risk to our financial systems. That's why we love this trade so much: the potential rewards are huge and the upfront costs still marginal. More importantly, it is a very good hedge against what would be a nightmare scenario for many financial institutions.

PART 3

Investment Implications

Some Preliminary Remarks On Investing

Our world of "accelerating creative destruction" and "acceleration phenomena" and "drastic policy changes" presents a daunting challenge to investors. So should we just give up on trying to figure out the growth trends reshaping the globe and simply put all of our money in a global equity index fund? Is the answer, as some argue, to throw our hands up, admit that the world is too complicated for us to understand, and entrust our capital to computers? I do not think so.

There is little doubt that indexation is the cheapest way of capturing the attractive long-term returns offered by the capitalistic system. From there, it would be easy to deduce that one should have part, if not all, of one's portfolio indexed. But this conclusion would be wrong, for indexation works on three basic premises, legitimate at the microeconomic level, but chaos-inducing on a macro scale. They are:

1. Active money managers allocate capital according to what they perceive to be the future marginal returns on invested capital (ROIC).

2. Few active (stock selection) money managers will outperform the indices over the long term.

3. Very few active money managers will add value through asset allocation. Massively diverging from indices does not work.

These three founding principles are fine on their own but **internally contradictory.** Indeed, the system can work only as long as active money managers attempt to do the job for which they are paid i.e., allocating capital according to what they perceive to be the future ROIC in the different investments which they consider at any given point in time. Most of them will fail, but the process of screening for future ROIC is vital for the well being of the capitalistic system. Winners emerge, losers collapse. In this creative destruction (or is it destructive creation?), capital is allocated efficiently through a constant system of trial and error.

To put it in another way: the active money managers (and their clients) support most of the costs; the indexers get most of the rewards. Without a doubt, this is what happened in the 1980s and 1990s. So why did it stop working? Easy. The active money managers, chastised by years of underperformance, were forced to become 'closet indexers'. In January 2000, some of our clients in the City got fired from their fund management jobs for refusing to own France Telecom or Nokia.

And this behaviour brought the entire system down. The business of money management had become so big after a decade-long bull market that it had been taken over by 'professional people', advised by consultants. Often, these management teams wanted to conserve, and not create. They were accountants, not entrepreneurs. The management of the firms (not money managers themselves anymore) attempted to reduce the unpredictability of the results of their money management teams by preventing them from taking risks. And risk was defined as a deviation from the index against which the money managers were measured (hence the introduction of 'risk controls', 'tracking errors' etc...).

What were the results of these changes? Initially, important changes in the industry. Later, a massive bear market. To put it succinctly, indexation became a victim of its own success for two reasons.

The first consequence of the move towards closet indexing was that money management evolved from being an exciting and intellectually stimulating business to a boring and mind-numbing number-crunching game. This was a blow to a number of individuals who had spent their lives in the industry; it also meant that money management started to attract a different type of character than it did a decade ago (i.e., originals, free-thinkers, crazy people…).

The second, most harmful consequence is that **capital started to be allocated according to size, rather than future returns on invested capital.** Indeed, relevant indices are all, for the most, part market-weighted. In simple English–which we don't always understand but profess to speak–this means that investments get allocated to companies according to their stock market size. This allocation of capital according to size was tried out before, and, the last time I checked, the Soviet Union was not doing that well.

Indeed, in an ironic twist of history, in its hour of triumph over communism, capitalism devised a **socialist** way of allocating capital. All of a sudden, investors all over the capitalist world decided that it was better to invest in companies according to their size then according to their marginal returns on invested capital. And the capital allocators did this supposedly for the benefit of workers (the future retirees). Unfortunately, if this system were pushed to its logical conclusion, the workers would be left holding the bag. As the Holy Catholic Church states, and history shows, the road to hell is paved with good intentions.

Behind this trend to allocating capital according to size, one finds hundreds of studies, published by thousands of scholars and consultants (and financed by Wall Street dollars) justifying indexation. But what the studies do not acknowledge is that the data on which conclusions are drawn represent a period where active management was both truly active and dominant. In other words, indexing represents a form of black box investing; but black box investing can only work if a) volumes are kept fairly low, b) nobody knows that a black box is operating (see the disaster behind the portfolio insurance of 1987) and c) nobody knows how the black box works. Clearly, none of these three rules applies to indexing.

The more money flows into indexation strategies, the more capital gets invested according to size, and the more capital is misallocated. This can only lead to a lower return on invested capital, which, in turn, can only lead to a lower growth rate and, more often than not, to huge disturbances in price levels. As the late 1990s craze showed, indexation is a guarantee for capital to be wasted, which automatically leads to lower growth and lower long-term returns on the stock markets. So we could have a very paradoxical result: indexers might keep outperforming but the long-term returns of the stock markets will fall, as a sign that the economy's structural growth rate is falling.

We need to remember Bastiat's law: 'there is always what you see and what you do not see'. **We shall see the underperformance of active money managers. We shall not understand the result of them being forced to index: the long term declines in the rates of returns in the stock markets.** A study of the 1998-2003 bull and bear markets illustrates perfectly what we are trying to prove. In 1999, we had the perfect case of a stock market going up strongly in the index because a few big stocks were bought massively by the indexers (which is fine), and then by the closet indexers (which is suicidal).

Being both a natural optimist and a fervent believer in an efficient free-market, I cannot believe that the system is bent on self-destruction. I do not want to admit that, because the money management industry has become too sophisticated and too risk averse for the good of the economic system it is supposed to serve, we will have to face years of bear markets and sub-par growth. The market will find a way to triumph. And in fact, it has. Indeed, as we all know, experienced money managers have been leaving the bigger firms in hordes over the past few years to set up their own hedge funds. Interestingly, the main characteristic of a hedge fund manager is that a) he aims to allocate capital efficiently, b) he can buy and sell pretty much what he likes and c) he sticks his neck out.

Very encouragingly, capital has flowed in huge amounts to this new breed of managers. By creating a class of absolute return oriented money managers, the system has effectively recreated the cautious money managers of yesteryear, bent on delivering steady and understandable returns. One hopes that the fellows willing to do their jobs (i.e. incur a high tracking error) will continue take to the cleaners the indexers and closet indexers. The more and the quicker they do it, the better for the long-term health of our economic systems.

Now of course, on this last point, I could be accused of singing from my own hymn-book. After all, my firm, GaveKal, has been a massive beneficiary of the growth in the hedge fund industry and today, some 40% of our research sales come from "hedge fund" clients. But the growth of the hedge fund industry has not only been a financial boon for GaveKal; indeed, our constant contacts with our hedge fund clients around the world have allowed us to better understand how different strategies can make money in different markets.

Breaking down the fields of hedge fund activity (merger arbitrage, convertible bond arbitrage, index arbitrage etc...) it seems to me that a typical hedge fund makes money in one of three ways (needless to say, a money manager is never limited in his choices. In fact, some of the best money managers I have met over the years usually play two, or even three of the below strategies at the same time):

1. 'Return to the Mean' Strategies: The first way to make money in the financial markets is to buy what is undervalued/oversold and to sell what is overvalued/overbought and wait for the asset price in question to return to its historical mean. This is the strategy adopted by most 'value' managers, but also frequently a number of 'macro-funds', 'distressed-debt', 'special-situations', etc...

2. Momentum Based Strategies: The second way to make money in the financial markets is to identify a trend and get in (and out) at the right time. Most money managers do try to follow momentum, but it is especially prevalent amongst 'growth' investors, 'macro-funds', and 'long/short' hedge funds.

3. Carry Trade Strategies: The third and final way to make money in the financial markets is to intelligently play the yield curve (i.e., borrow at low rates and lend at higher rates…and hope that the markets remain continuous.). Most of the 'arbitrage' type of hedge funds run some kind of carry trade.

Reviewing this dichotomy with my missed friend Hunt Taylor (a man who could forget more about hedge funds in a day than I could hope to learn in a lifetime), Hunt told me: "and remember, the carry-trade strategies tend to eat like birds and shit like cows"! To put it more politely, one could say that a lot of the carry-trade strategies "pick up nickels in front of a steam-roller" and that, unfortunately, every now and then one gets steam-rolled.

This conversation with Hunt came back to my memory this summer on the news that many "quant" hedge funds, and funds that had been making money selling volatility, were facing the worst month in their history. For me, this illustrated a simple truth, in periods of endogenous tensions (see Chapter 2), carry-trade strategies offer poor diversification for a portfolio. In fact, in periods of endogenous tensions, it is often better to have "negative carry-trades" on as those can often offer tremendous protection.

This much has been clear in recent months. Think about how long positions in the Yen helped save portfolios returns in August and November 2007. Or how buying protection on sub-prime debt helped Paulson, but also my friends Kyle Bass (of Hayman Capital) and Mark Hart (of Corriente Capital), post returns in 2007 that were beyond impressive.

It thus follows that carry can be a dangerous game. The rule should be to look for positive carry in the most uncrowded of areas and to accept negative-carry in the areas where an endogenous shock is possible because of recent excesses.

So what are today's momentum, return to the mean, positive carry and negative carry trades? Or, in other words, how is my own portfolio structured?

Momentum Trade #1: The Growth in Asian & Middle-Eastern Consumption

In a recent conversation with my friend Kenneth Hung, one of the best money managers I have had the good luck to meet, I happened to expand on the merits of a particular Japanese equity market strategy. Kenneth very politely replied: "that sounds very interesting. But I like to bat downhill wickets. It's just easier to make money that way".

And, of course, Kenneth was right (in the end, I did lose money on this particular Japanese trade). As an investor, it is essential to identify what the structural trends are and: a) stay on top of these trends until they turn or reach valuations that imply a very crowded trade and b) avoid diversifying in assets that do not have a good positive tailwind. Otherwise, this may not be diversification but "diworsification"....

In the previous chapter, we identified a number of trends but at this stage, none seems as obvious as the continued solid growth in Asian and Middle-Eastern consumption. Indeed, we should expect consumption in our part of the world to remain strong thanks to:

- Sustained currency revaluations (this always favors the consumer and penalizes the producer)

- The acceleration phenomena

- Collapses in distribution costs as infrastructure improves

- Demographic transition in a number of countries

　Accelerating urban migration

- Greater female participation in the workforce

Now how do we play this in the financial markets? One obvious answer is, of course, to err on the long side on all Asian and Middle-Eastern currencies. Another answer is to continue to overweight stocks linked to the consumer in those areas. Yet another answer is to keep buying what the Asians themselves will want to buy (mostly food, precious metals, and energy but also fine wines, art etc…). Though for me, the best answer is probably to keep buying high-end real estate across Asia.

Let's review these various "derivative plays" on Asian and Middle-Eastern consumption individually:

A. Buying Asian and Middle-Eastern Currencies

Undeniably, one of the more important questions confronting investors today is the question of the US$. If we are right about the impending change in monetary policies across Asia and the Middle-East, will the US$ continue collapsing? Will it remain the world's reserve currency? Will it survive the extremely well-documented profligacy of the US consumer/implosion in US real estate/empire overstretch, etc (insert your favourite perma-bear lament here)?…

As we look at it, a currency has historically had three functions: 1) a store of value, 2) a standard of value, and 3) a means of exchange. Now, as it turns out, other currencies compete with the US on these attributes, but none competes with the US on all three. Specifically:

1. **A store of value:** In recent years, we have found that a number of currencies met investors' needs as "stores of value": the Euro, Swiss Franc, and Sterling have, by and large, been very efficient "stores of value" for the world. We will thus call these three currencies the "savings currencies".

2. **A standard of value:** When one talks about standards of value, one usually refers to gold (everyone knows the story of how an ounce of gold has, through time, bought a decent suit) or a basket of currencies. So on that front, it makes sense to look at the US$ against commodity currencies, such as the Canadian, Australian or New Zealand dollars, the Norwegian Krona, or the South African Rand.

3. **A means of exchange:** On this front, it makes sense to compare the US$ against the currencies of the countries with which the US trade deficit has, in recent years, been rising the fastest, namely the RMB, JPY, KRW, MXP, SG$, HK$ but also the Middle-Eastern currencies (dirham, dinar etc...)

Putting it all together, we could say that we have three US$ exchange rates upon which to focus: a) US$ vs. savings currencies (Euro, GBP, CHF), b) US$ vs. commodity currencies (AU$, NZ$, CA$, ZAR, NOK) and c) US$ vs. trading currencies (SG$, RMB, JPY, MXP, HK$...). **And all of these three exchange rates have behaved very differently.**

Indeed, as illustrated by the chart below, from 1993 to 2001, we had the mother of all revaluations of the US$ against all three currency functions.

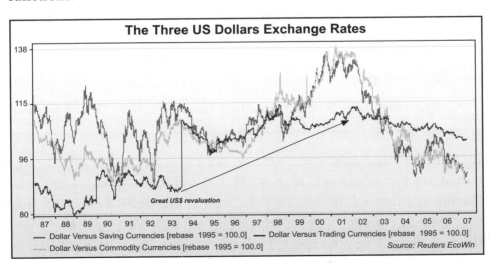

The Three US Dollars Exchange Rates

—— Dollar Versus Saving Currencies [rebase 1995 = 100.0]   —— Dollar Versus Trading Currencies [rebase 1995 = 100.0]
—— Dollar Versus Commodity Currencies [rebase 1995 = 100.0]
Source: Reuters EcoWin

However, since then, we have experienced a massive devaluation of the US currency against the "commodity currencies" (which makes sense given the rally in commodities and the fact that interest rates in commodity producing countries have tended to be higher than elsewhere, thereby attracting foreign capital). The US$ is also at a low against the "savings currencies". But interestingly, against the "trading currencies", the US$ had not, until recently, experienced much of a devaluation. This is truly surprising since the main reason for the US$ weakness (or so we have been told) is the massive US current account deficit. So, in good logic, the "trading currencies" should have moved higher.

Of course, the "trading currencies" did not rise because, as mentioned above, they were manipulated by central banks (whether the PBoC, the MAS, the HKMA…) and because interest rates there were too low (Japan, Taiwan…). Moreover, in a bid to maintain their currencies at undervalued levels, the central banks of the "trading currencies" have not only been buying US$, but also "commodity" and "savings" currencies in large size.

But what happens if, as looks increasingly likely, the Asian central banks start to change their monetary policies and no longer prevent their currencies from rising against the US$? Then:

- Asian and Middle-Eastern central banks will no longer be producing vast amounts of domestic excess liquidity. In turn this excess liquidity may stop flowing into commodities as it has done in recent years.

- Asian and Middle-Eastern central banks will have less reserves to redeploy into Euro, GBP or CHF deposits.

Or to put it differently: there were no fundamental reasons for "savings currencies' to rise as much as they did in the past few years. Except one: "savings currencies" were taking the adjustment against the US$ that the "trading currencies" were refusing to take. But if this is no longer the case, should we not expect "trading currencies" to soar, and "savings currencies" to tank?

B. Buying Equities Linked to the Asian and Middle Eastern Consumers

In our discussions with clients, it is obvious that most investors want to be bullish Asian and Middle-Eastern equities. After all, everyone can see the impressive rises in living standards and economic activity currently unfolding around the region. Still, our smarter clients usually bring up three very legitimate concerns to temper our enthusiasm on Asian equities. These are:

After a five year bull market, valuations on Asian equities are rather stretched. This is a valid concern though it could easily be argued that Asia sports both very expensive (China A-shares, Indian large-caps…) and very inexpensive markets (Thailand, Taiwan, even HK small caps following the bloodbath of the August 2007-March 2008 sell-off). In fact, we are not so sure that thinking of Asian markets as either "cheap" or "expensive" is that useful. After all, as investors, we invest in companies; and today, we can still find plenty of interesting companies, with exciting stories to tell, trading at acceptable valuations.

Of course, finding these companies means being on the ground and doing some hard work… although in the coming year, the typical Asian equity investor may end up doing very well simply because he has been doing so poorly in the recent past! Indeed, imagine a lazy investor. A year ago, our investor realizes that Asia is the main growth driver of the world and concludes that he needs more Asian names in his portfolio. Unfortunately, however, he knows little about Asian companies and thus decides to build himself a portfolio around Asia's strongest companies and biggest brand names.

In Japan, our investor buys Sony, Canon, Matsushita and Toyota. In Hong Kong, he buys HSBC, Li & Fung, Hutchinson Whampoa and Cheung Kong. In Singapore, he buys DBS and Singapore Airlines. In Taiwan, he buys TSMC, UMC and Hon Hai. In India, he buys Infosys, Dr Reddy's, Tata Consultancy and Satyam Systems. In Korea, he buys

Samsung Electronics, Kookmin Bank and Hyundai Motors. In China, he buys Lenovo and China Mobile....

Looking at the Asian boom, he feels quietly confident about his portfolio, though, unfortunately, when he picks up his broker's statement today, he notices that, on most of the names above, he is actually losing money... and this despite a raging bull market in Asian equities!

In the chart below, we aggregate the above names in a common "Asian brand name" index and found that, since April 2007, the relative performance of Asia's biggest names has literally fallen out of bed. And to some extent, this makes sense. Buying Asia's "big brands" was a flawed strategy for the past two years, since these companies have large international exposures, and investors into Asia were keen to increase exposure to "Asian pure plays".

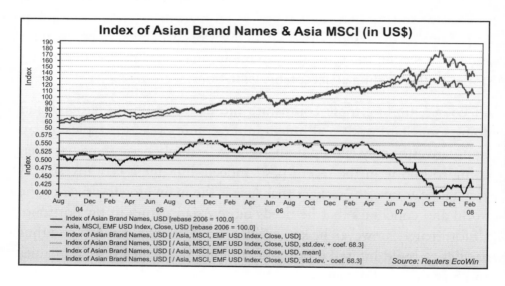

However, today, the valuation gap between "Asia's brands" and the "pure plays" is really starting to yawn. For example, does it make sense for DBS and HSBC to trade at 1.5x-1.8x book value while China's Bank of Communications currently trades at 5.4x book? So if nothing else, investors can today buy Asia's main brands on the cheap (and by the way, one can also throw into that mix the OECD big brand names like

LVMH or AIG, which do so much business in Asia but which, for the past few quarters, have not exactly set the world on fire either.)

Asian equities have historically offered poor returns over the long-term.

This argument, which is less an argument than a statement of a fact, is of course very problematic for investors in Asian equities. As an emerging-market equity manager once put it to me: **there is no single four year period since 1982 in which Asian equities have outperformed Latin American equities.** And this despite the fact that Asia's economies have grown by leaps and bounds and massively outperformed Latin American economies.

So why is this? Are the managers of Asian businesses so bad that they can not generate profits in the midst of massive economic expansion? Are Latin American managers so good as to simply beat the socks-off their Asian counterparts? I do not think so. In fact, the explanation may be a lot simpler: as mentioned in Chapter 11, the savings rate across most Asian countries is extremely high. Meanwhile, in Latin American most wealthy individuals have historically tended to redirect their savings as far away from their domestic economies as possible (buying apartments in Miami, Madrid, etc...). It was the Conquistador mentality: Latin America was a place where one came to make money, not keep money! As a result, capital in Latin America over the past twenty five years has come at a healthy premium; investors willing to take the "Latam risk" where richly rewarded by companies starved of capital to finance their expansion. The same, of course, can not be said of Asia where capital, being more plentiful, did not need to be as richly rewarded. One of our bets, of course, is that this has changed and that capital in both Asia and Latin America is now almost as equally available. Still, given the past twenty-five years of track record, this is a bold bet to make... which is why one must play the boom in Asian consumption through other vehicles besides simply the equity markets.

C. Are Commodities the Answer?

There is little doubt that, over the past five years, exposure to commodities has been one of the best ways to participate in the Asian growth story. But will it remain so for the future? In the near term, the answer is most likely 'Yes'. Indeed, everywhere we care to look in the commodity space, we find supply constraints linked to lacks of qualified personnel, environmental restrictions, delays in getting the necessary equipment, etc... Meanwhile, the demand side, thanks to the acceleration phenomena in the emerging markets, is not abating that rapidly.

But having said that, over the longer-term, the short-term difficulties of bringing on extra supply and the possibility of continued demand do not guarantee that commodities will continue heading to the moon. After all, imagine for a second that we are in 1946 and that I describe to you a world of air-conditioners, neon lights, electrical appliances, computers, jet airplanes, pleasure yachts, three car garages and the SUVs that go in them... Imagine that I also show you how the world will grow from a total population of 1.5bn people to 6.5bn people... Imagine then that, in my great foresight, I see how central banks will lose the plots, allow monetary aggregates to explode, move everyone to fiat-money, etc...

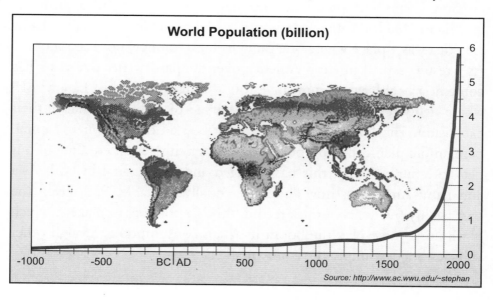

World Population (billion)

Source: http://www.ac.wwu.edu/~stephan

Then you and I would have probably agreed that the best thing to own would have been commodities. In fact, we probably would have wanted to own nothing but commodities!

However, adjusted for inflation, commodities would have been one of the worst investments we could have made. Indeed, despite a boom in growth, the CRB index adjusted for inflation (see chart below) has had dismal returns.

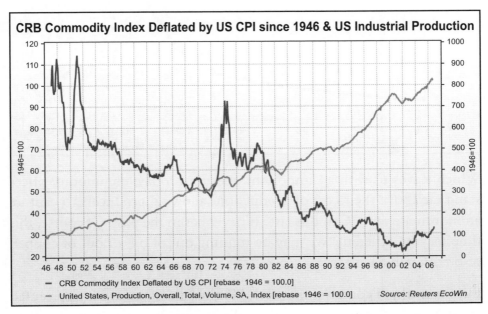

CRB Commodity Index Deflated by US CPI since 1946 & US Industrial Production

- CRB Commodity Index Deflated by US CPI [rebase 1946 = 100.0]
- United States, Production, Overall, Total, Volume, SA, Index [rebase 1946 = 100.0]   *Source: Reuters EcoWin*

So why, despite the great fundamental environment, did commodities fare so poorly? And what should we expect now that the growth rate of the global population is slowing, and even shrinking in most of the world's richer countries (Japan, Germany, Italy, Russia...)?

The answer is of course that commodities over the very long-term tend to return to their marginal cost of production. And that thanks to technology, freer trade, lack of full-scale wars, etc... the marginal cost of production of almost all commodities has spent the past fifty years falling.

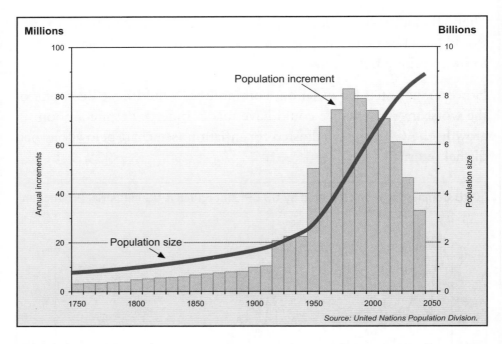

Millions   Billions

Source: United Nations Population Division.

Which leaves us with an important question: today, commodity prices stand far above their cost of production (allowing producers to capture an inordinate rent). Can this last? It never has in the past. Of course, this time may be different. We may be running out of oil, or out of copper, or out of arable land...

But the truth, of course, is that such Malthusian arguments are presented at every single commodity bull market... and they always turn out to be wrong for several reasons. Firstly, Malthusian theories fail to capture the economic impact of rising prices as drivers of efficiency gains in the extraction process and as incentives to deploy more capital into exploration and production. In other words, Malthusian arguments work solely on the extrapolation of past trends into the future. But the whole point of changes in market prices is to send signals to both consumers and producers to alter their behavior. And the massive rise in commodity prices over the past five years is just such a signal! Secondly, using past trends for guidance also completely fails to capture advances in technology. And it is these advances in technology (Schumpeterian creative destruction) which distinguish capitalism from all other economic systems.

So our take on commodities is a simple one: we fully understand, and admire, our clients who are willing to make the bet that the Asian demand and the current supply constraint can only mean higher prices. It undeniably feels as if, in the short term, they will be right. As illustrated in the chart below, most commodities continue to make new highs.

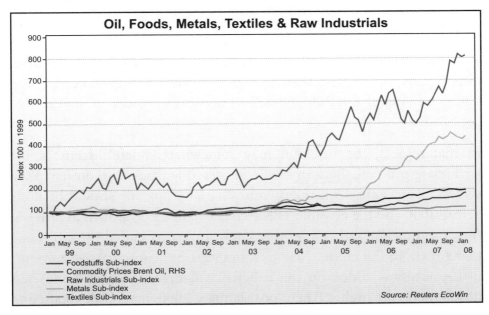

Source: Reuters EcoWin

But at some point, capitalism's structural trends will prevail and commodities will return to their marginal cost of production. This point may not happen for years. Though, in the near term, we do fear a potential "inventory correction" linked to the Chinese Olympics.

It is no secret that China views the 2008 Beijing Games as its "coming-out in modern society" party. As such, China will not want to present to the world the image of polluted air and clogged-up traffic that we reviewed in Chapter 12. Which brings me to 1995 and the days when Beijing was hosting the world's "International Women's Day" (which included a visit from Hillary Clinton). At the time, to portray a "clean image", a number of factories around Beijing were ordered to shut down and, sure enough, the skies turned blue.

Will we see the same thing this time around for the Olympics? Given that the whole world's attention will be on China, it is likely that the government will do all that is in its power (and that's a lot), to ensure that the events in Beijing, Qingdao (sailing), Shanghai (soccer) and Hong Kong (equestrian) will not be spoiled by pollution. It may be that a number of factories are simply ordered to shut down for up to three months.

Facing this threat, it would make sense for producers in China to "double-order" parts, or even finished goods. One will not want to come into China on August 8th 2008 (at 8PM!) needing an order of anything to get filled!

In that respect, the situation may somewhat be reminiscent of the tech space pre-Y2K. Back in 1998-99, everyone loaded up on new PCs, servers, routers etc... on the premise that any upgrade should be done before 2000 and the possible Y2K tech crash. In 1999, growth in tech was thus magnificent and, as we now know, investors ended up projecting that growth to the moon. New factories were built and massive amounts of capacity was added on the belief that demand for tech goods was now structurally higher. Then, post January 2000, inventories started to appear all over the place, and prices collapsed.

As it turns out, inventories in China are no longer growing at their usual 10-15% annual pace (i.e.: in line with nominal GDP) but are instead growing at a 30%-40% annual clip. Is this because industrialists are piling in six months of production into nine? And, if so, is the market being sent the wrong signal (and acting on that signal)? If so, could we not suffer a typical "inventory adjustment" cycle after the Olympics? At this stage, for us, this has to be the biggest immediate risk for raw materials.

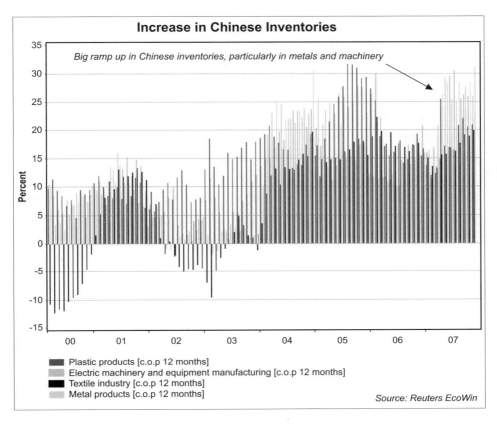

Increase in Chinese Inventories

Big ramp up in Chinese inventories, particularly in metals and machinery

- Plastic products [c.o.p 12 months]
- Electric machinery and equipment manufacturing [c.o.p 12 months]
- Textile industry [c.o.p 12 months]
- Metal products [c.o.p 12 months]

Source: Reuters EcoWin

D. Is Asian Real Estate the Answer?

As mentioned above, the investor who twenty-five years ago placed his savings in Asian equities has massively underperformed his Latin-American counterpart. But the opposite is true of the investor who bought real estate in Hong Kong, Singapore, Kuala Lumpur, Shanghai or Bangkok against the one who bought Rio, Buenos Aires, Santiago and Caracas. While Asia's excess of capital may have prevented handsome returns on equities, it definitely helped propel local real estate markets higher.

Combining all of the trends mentioned above, the coming Asian currency revaluation (which should lead to even lower real rates across the region and higher disposable incomes), the demographic transition, the urban migration, the increase in the standards of living, the growth in financial products… We see no reason to believe why Asian real estate should start doing badly.

So to conclude this long chapter, it is obvious that there are many ways to skin a cat and that investors can find many different options to play the near certain expansion in Asian consumption. At this juncture, my preferred way is to buy Asian real estate, Asian equities linked to domestic consumption and remain as long Asian currencies as I possibly can. Of course, this is also where my comfort zone is the highest. Meanwhile, some GaveKal clients feel far more comfortable playing the Asian consumption boom through the commodity markets. Others still by buying US and EMU exporters into the Asian Boom. All these strategies have worked well in the past few years and I want to hope that the momentum is still with us.

Momentum Trade #2: Dealing With the Shortages–the Infrastructure Boom Continues

As mentioned above, the world today is facing various supply constraints, especially, though not only, in the raw material space. All too often across the emerging world, telecom and transport infrastructure are nowhere near a level which would be considered adequate in the 21st century. The same can be said of food or energy distribution…

Take the current storms in China which, over the Chinese New Year holidays, stranded tens of millions of passengers for days on jammed railway lines. As millions stayed for weeks in towns without electricity, running water, or food delivery, the situation became critical enough to warrant a policy change from the Chinese leadership. Indeed, given the recent debacle, China's policymakers are worried about large-scale public dissatisfaction with their leaders. And as the harsh weather underlined the faults in China's infrastructure grid, the government reacted by announcing that new investment funds had been approved to direct investments into more infrastructure. After all, we should not forget that China's leaders are first and foremost engineers. So when confronting a problem, their natural instinct is to build something.

Now for all our talk about the "Asian infrastructure boom", we are sometimes accused of making a bigger deal out of a boom which has, thus far, been mostly a Chinese affair. And to be fair, a large majority of the Asian infrastructure spending (roads, telecoms, harbours…) of recent years has by and large taken place in just one country (China). Other hotbeds of population growth (Thailand, Indonesia, the Philippines, India, Vietnam…) have thus far mostly been bypassed in the great construction and capital spending unleashed of recent years; at least, that much is clear to anyone hoping to make more than four meetings in one day in Mumbai, Jakarta or Manila.

Now why has infrastructure spending lagged so badly in the above countries? We find a number of reasons:

- Political processes have suffered from gridlock and politicians have been unable to come through with infrastructure spending plans. This fact has lately been garnering media attention in India—but Thailand, Indonesia, the Philippines and other countries have also suffered from politicians' weak hands.

- Following the Financial Crisis, interest rates in the more "sporty" Asian nations were very high. And they only started to come down about two years ago.

- Also following the crisis, Asian currencies remained massively undervalued for a long while. And this undervaluation prevented a number of countries from buying the expensive machine tools (produced by Japan, Germany, Sweden, the US...) necessary to undergo serious infrastructure work.

In other words, following the Asian Crisis, the more "fringe" Asian countries found that a) their cost of capital was too high to justify any kind of capital spending, b) they couldn't afford the machines anyway and c) the politicians did not have the power to push through large spending plans. As a result, imports of machinery never really recovered to their pre '97 highs, cement manufacturers underperformed and traffic jams around the major cities only got worse.

The exciting thing today is that, all of these trends have started to roll over. Interest rates around the region are falling; exchange rates are rising and, most importantly, the cost of machine tools is plummeting as China is transforming itself into a net exporter of machine tools. This means that countries can now dig up earth, build roads or fill in harbors at a much lower cost thanks to Chinese machines.

This last point is an important one for it will likely help unleash a secondary deflationary influence around the world. Indeed, think of the plight of the textile manufacturer in Bangladesh today. He has cheap workers but cannot afford the expensive machinery produced by the US, Japan or Germany. So the productivity of his firm is low. But now, thanks to the cheap machines produced in China, he will soon churn out ten times as many T-shirts per employee as he used to a year ago. So one bet is sure: whatever goods come out of these Chinese-made, recently exported machines will not be going up in price!

With the confluence of these forces, we expect infrastructure spending in Asia, the Middle-East and elsewhere around the world to continue rising. This will be great news for local cement producers, steel producers, but also local supermarkets and other distributors who stand to benefit from greater ease, and lower costs in moving goods.

In fact, it seems to us that an increase in infrastructure spending will soon be seen as akin to tech spending in the late 1990s. Back then, if our reader remembers, the argument presented was that companies had no choice but to invest in tech… even if they had no money to do so! If they did not invest in tech, they were doomed to fail. Today, the same argument can be made for countries and infrastructure spending. The emerging markets that do not at least make a valiant effort in keeping up with China in terms of infrastructure will have a challenging time seeing any kind of rapid economic growth.

Incidentally, this theme of global infrastructure spending regroups nicely our four structural "megatrends", in that the financial revolution helps finance projects all around the world, the growth in the emerging markets makes such projects a necessity, globalization and the emergence of the platform company model makes them financially viable, while their emergence only amplifies further the acceleration in creative destruction. If only for these reasons, we would not be surprised if infrastructure plays thus end up as the next "bubble"!

Return to Mean Trade 1: Buying Up "Tools", especially Technology

According to classic economic theory, a good can either have a value because it is beautiful (e.g.: a jewel, gold), or because it is useful (e.g.: a tool, a software program). In the first case, it is customary to say that the good's value comes from scarcity. In the second case, the value comes from increased efficiency. Needless to say, both sources of value are quoted in the financial markets. In fact, this is the market's purpose. Why do we highlight this point? Every two weeks, our colleague Clay Allen (_www.clayallen.com_) publishes a study of the best performing twenty sectors on the S&P 500, on a rolling three-month basis. Lately, these reports have shown a rare polarisation between the two different sources of value. Indeed, excluding the sectors that managers buy in periods of uncertainty (tobacco, staples...), we find that the market is split right down the middle between scarcity and efficiency.

- **In the scarcity camp:** farm products, non-metallic mineral mining, oil and gas, silver, oil and gas refining, dairy products, iron & steel.

- **In the efficiency camp:** agricultural chemicals, internet service and information providers, multimedia, hospitals, telephone services, farm machinery, diversified electronics, and application software.

Once again, capitalism is facing the challenge of Malthusian scarcity, which encourages government intervention to "allocate the scarcity fairly". This time around however, the scarcity is being triggered by the growth in developing markets (China, India, etc...) and the consequent rise in demand for commodities, whether hard or soft. And, as always, capitalism is reacting as it should and a familiar chain of events is unfolding:

1. The prices of the underlying scarce assets skyrocket to levels way above the marginal cost of production.

2. As a result, exceptional margins start to appear for those who can produce the scarce good (in today's case, commodities).

3. A mad scramble starts to increase the production of the scarce good (to capture the exceptional rent).

4. Simultaneously, a lot of money is invested to find a substitute to the scarce products (witness the performance of anything related to alternative energy) or boost productivity (check out Monsanto's impressive performance).

5. Usually, at some point, somebody somewhere comes up with what is commonly called a "disruptive technology", which materially changes either the supply or the demand of the scarce goods.

6. As a result, the margins of producing scarcity assets return to more normal levels, sometimes in quite a dramatic fashion.

7. Finally, scarcity assets come back down to the level dictated by the new marginal cost of production.

Let us give an example: everybody knows that the problem with a windmill is that the energy cannot be stored. The technology for batteries does not allow it (and probably never will). However, engineers in the US are now starting to build windmills on top of underground cavities. The idea is to put a turbine at the bottom of the windmill and start compressing the air around the windmill down into the cavity. When energy is needed, one lets the compressed air back into the turbine to create electricity, and then divert this electricity into the electric grid. In other words, all of a sudden, a solution has been found to store the wind.

The higher oil prices go, the more convinced we become that the 21st century will be the century of electricity, not of oil. As we mentioned above, we firmly believe that capitalism will, once again, break through the Malthusian doomsday scenarios. The only question is not if, but when - and through which technologies? Over the past few years, the market has been very busy bidding up "jewels" and not caring much for "tools". In a sense, this is the mirror image of what happened between 1995 and 2000. Back then, the market only wanted "tools" but an investor who loaded up on "jewels" is laughing today... Is now the time to make the switch back?

The timing on this question is both essential and difficult. In recent weeks, the behavior of the markets has been anything but normal and one could not avoid the feeling that a massive bout of 'forced selling" was taking place. Now forced selling can occur for a variety of reasons. It can either be triggered by:

- **A player in the system with too much leverage on wrong positions.** We had a perfect example of this last summer when the "quant" hedge funds had to get out of illiquid positions. Another example was the 1998 LTCM blow-up.

- **A panic by the public and a sell-off of their mutual funds holdings.** The mutual funds then have to sell to pay for the redemptions. This is what happened following the 9/11 terrorist attacks.

- **A major market participant is hit by its own regulatory environment.** And here we usually find the insurance industry. In the last six months of 1974, we saw furious selling of stocks by UK insurance companies (which led to the Bank of England's "lifeboat operation"). We also saw this in the second half of 2002 (which incidentally marked the time to get into "jewels").

Today, and as mentioned above (see chapter 2), it would seem that we have returned to this sort of forced selling again. And so, the markets have to absorb an avalanche of sell orders which have absolutely nothing to do with the economy or corporate earnings, and everything to do with the fact that insurance companies are breaching their reserve requirements and have no choice but to sell equities and buy bonds. This happens regardless of the prices reached by the equities or the government bonds! Simply because of regulations, capital is misallocated on a grand scale.

Needless to say, where there is misallocation of capital, there is also an opportunity. And for our readers that do not suffer from the attention of the regulators, that do not have time constraints, and for whom the end of the year is nothing but a sad reminder that they are getting older, then equities today represent extraordinary value. In the last few months, we have had an enormous amount of forced selling, which has artificially depressed the prices of the shares that pension funds once owned (i.e. those that were in the index, namely the big caps and the mega caps).

Sometimes, investing may be no more than taking the other side of the transactions imposed on pension funds and insurance companies by the regulators and the consultants. Today, minimizing cash and fixed income exposures and maximizing equities is a way to sell short the consultants and the regulators. This is a return to the mean trade that we like.

Positive Carry-Trade # 1: Buying Up Japanese REITS.

With the 'Livedoor scandal' in 2006, Japanese equity markets basically lost their main driver: the hope that shareholder activism would push Japan's placid managers into delivering higher returns for shareholders. Since then, Japanese equities have been extremely lacklustre and most foreign investors have scratched their heads as to what could be the "catalyst" leading to a Japanese re-rating. With the political situation deteriorating, with Japan moving back into deflation, with global growth decelerating, with earnings growth in Japan likely to come under pressure because of the higher Yen, foreign investors have, in recent months, increasingly thrown in the towel and walked away from this perennial underperformer. As everyone knows by now, Japan faces two main problems:

1) Japanese policy-makers continue to show an uncanny ability to shoot themselves in the foot. For example, not satisfied with the fact that the 2006 controls on the consumer finance industry nearly pushed the country into recession, the government, in 2007, imposed a new building code which will ensure that construction plummets and probably takes out around 1% of Japanese GDP growth (1% that Japan doesn't really have to spare today!)

2) Japanese banks have, for all intents and purposes, simply not been lending. And without loan growth, it is hard to see economic activity accelerate or asset prices increase a lot.

This last point was made absolutely clear at a recent lunch hosted by a Japanese REIT listed in Singapore. We asked the question of how much leverage the REIT took, and who provided the leverage. The answer, we felt, was surprising. We were told that the leverage hovered between 45% and 65%, and that even at such low gearing levels, Japanese local banks were very reluctant to lend. Instead, the REIT borrowed at 2%-3% from well-known, large, American investment banks. These investment banks then repackaged the loans and sold them onto Japanese banks for a little over half the yield.

Of course, the Japanese banks then ended up with pretty much the same risk (and lower returns) as if they had done the loan directly; but now, instead of having a loan on their book that says "building in Fukuoka", the Japanese banker has a nice paper with a "big leading investment bank" stamp on it. And this made them feel better about their risk. However, with American banks (i.e.: Citi, Bear…) now forced to go cap in hand to recapitalize damaged balance sheets, could the Japanese banks start to think that paying half the yield away on a loan in order to get a nice stamp of approval from guys with devastated balance sheets is not such a great trade after all? That, if they are going to carry the end-risk (which, as owners of structured products everywhere are finding out, are greater than they expected), then they may as well capture more of the returns? As these realizations dawn on Japanese banks, will they stop sitting on their hands and start lending again? In fact, this may have started: last year for the first time since 1991, the Japanese banking multiplier appears to be decisively in positive territory:

Interestingly, Japanese banks must surely be the only banks in the world not underperforming their market! One of our rules is to feel good about Japan when banks are outperforming; and this is now happening.

With the opportunities of plowing money abroad fast disappearing (foreign equities and structured products are not very attractive to volatility-relunctant Japanese investors, while foreign government bonds no longer offer yields attractive enough to warrant taking the foreign

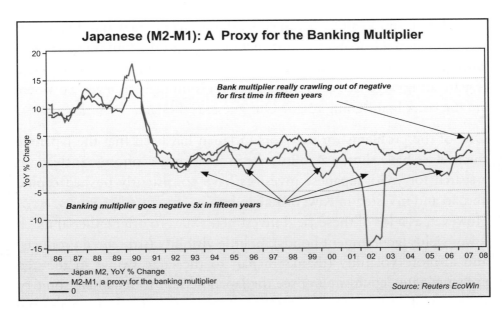

Japanese (M2-M1): A Proxy for the Banking Multiplier

Bank multiplier really crawling out of negative for first time in fifteen years

Banking multiplier goes negative 5x in fifteen years

Japan M2, YoY % Change
M2-M1, a proxy for the banking multiplier
0

Source: Reuters EcoWin

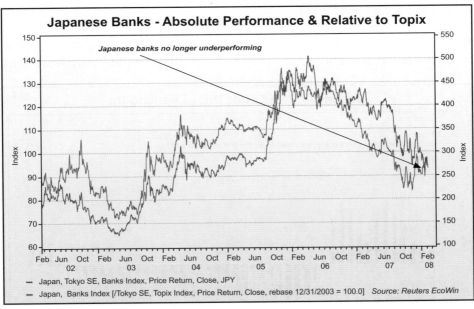

Japanese Banks - Absolute Performance & Relative to Topix

Japanese banks no longer underperforming

— Japan, Tokyo SE, Banks Index, Price Return, Close, JPY
— Japan, Banks Index [/Tokyo SE, Topix Index, Price Return, Close, rebase 12/31/2003 = 100.0]   *Source: Reuters EcoWin*

exchange risk), could it be that the US-centered credit crunch is finally pushing Japanese banks to once again lend to domestics? But, if so, to whom? After all, thanks to last year's government interference in the consumer finance industry, lending to consumers at high interest rates is now close to impossible. Meanwhile, thanks to the new building codes recently adopted, loans to construction are sure to plummet. Finally, with global growth slowing, Japan's corporate sector (which by and large is generating large free cash-flows anyway) is unlikely to lever. So where are the bank loans going to go? Our guess: real estate.

One of the problems for investors in Japan has been that the Japanese themselves have shown zero interest in their own economy. Instead, in a search for yield, Japanese investors have consistently pushed capital abroad and invested in Kiwi or Italian bonds, structured products, etc... However, as a lot of these yield investments start to offer either a) much lower yields (government bonds), b) little visibility (structured products) and c) more volatility (thanks in part to the large swings in the Yen exchange rate), could we not see the Japanese start to repatriate some of their capital. In fact, is this not what is happening today and explains the recent rapid rise in the Yen?

Of course, we are still left with the question of where this capital will go once it has made its way back home? After all, it could easily head back

Source: Reuters EcoWin

straight under the mattress. Or, it could start to look domestically for the yield that it can no longer safely get abroad. And on this note, it is important to note that Japanese real estate, for the first time since 1990, has been showing four consecutive quarters of higher prices. In fact, real estate now seems to be one of the few places in Japan where one can get yield somewhat safely.

The fact that the government's new measures will, grind new construction down to a halt makes existing real estate all the more attractive. Indeed, while the government's new measures is terrible news for GDP growth, they also mean that very little new supply will make its way unto the market in the next 24 months.

Now interestingly, despite all of the above developments (bank loans picking up, real estate prices no longer falling, higher Yen, etc...) Japanese REITS have shed−50% since June 1st and are now offering yields of anywhere between 4% and 8%, i.e.: yields high enough to entice the more risk averse Japanese investors.

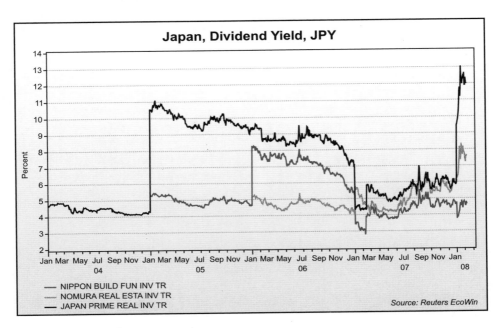

For the past two years, we have advised our clients to stay away from the Japanese market but we are increasingly starting to feel that Japanese REITs and other high dividend-paying Japanese plays present a compelling story. A positive carry-trade in Yen? This provides attractive diversification for our portfolios!

Negative Carry-Trade # 1: Buying Up Protection on the Real Fat Tail Risk in the System: the Possibility that the EMU Breaks Down

In Japan, when the economy slowed after the 1990 bust, the government stepped in and its spending went through the roof. The government issued a lot of JGBs to finance its spending. And, conveniently, if the market looked like it might not want extra JGBs, the BoJ was there to absorb them. Throughout the late 1990's, we saw the BoJ time and again intervening in the markets to ensure that yields remained low.

Now as we write, it seems that the slowdown is unfolding across Europe and that the credit crunch is already starting to have an impact on the price that the various European governments have to pay to borrow. So the question needs to be asked about what happens next? Will the Italian government be able to tell the ECB to buy its bonds? Remember that Italy has repeatedly been in breach of its treaty obligations (i.e.: no deficit higher than –3% of GDP) and that the ECB is most unlikely to look kindly on any request Italy might present.

In 2001, the Argentine government could not tell the US Fed to print more money in order to roll-over its debt and so Argentina went bust. Japan was always able to tell the BoJ to print Yen and buy JGBs, and so ten-year Japanese yields fell to 0.42%.

Today, the whole of the sovereign debt of Italy has been issued in a currency which is not under the control of the Italian Ministry of Finance. Nor is there a European Ministry of Finance. So, in a crisis, either the ECB decides to play nice, and buy everybody's government bonds, in which case interest rates fall (and the Euro tanks). Or the ECB decides to stick to its mandate, in which case real interest rates rise, the Euro shoots up and activity in Europe implodes.

So which way will the ECB lean? The question is not academic. Today, Italy has a debt to GDP equivalent of 105%. If interest rates on that debt are at 3.5% and the nominal GDP grows at 2% (as it does today after a period of global synchronized boom) then an increasing part of the Italian GDP is being captured simply to service the debt. Moreover, if nominal rates compound in Italy at 3.5% and nominal GDP compounds at 2%, then one does not need a Nobel Prize in economics to deduct that, at some point, bankruptcy is unavoidable; the "awesome power" of compounding interest rates must lead to an Italian bankruptcy. This only accelerates if GDP falls to 0%.

On the intra-European comparisons, if, in Austria, interest rates are at 3.5%, but nominal growth is at 5.5%, the debt burden of Austria will keep falling, (while it will keep rising in Italy). This should lead to a massive opening in spreads between the good signatures (Austria, Holland, etc…) and the bad signatures (Italy, Greece, etc…). This means that the cost of capital will go up in Italy, and down in Austria. All things being equal, capital spending should then collapse in Italy and go through the roof in Austria. Unemployment should explode in Italy and contract massively in Austria, etc… Incidentally, is this what we have now started to witness?

Of course, massive divergences in costs of capital and availability of labor have occurred within countries throughout history (i.e.: differences between southeast and northeast England) and have not always led to implosion. In fact, differences in growth typically lead to population migrations (i.e.: if people can't find jobs in Michigan, they move to California).

But will the Italians move en masse to Austria? Will the Germans move to Holland? Given that most European countries' population are getting older, that seems unlikely. Indeed, immigration is a thing that young people do (though we do love the story of the 93-year-old

Jewish grandmother immigrating to the US from Germany in 1934 who, when asked by the customs official why she was immigrating at such an advanced age, replied: "there is no future for me in Germany"). Older folks tend to get set in their ways and do not move around.

The other option for Europe to harmonize the differences in economic growth is to tax the wealth creating regions, and re-distribute the money to the wealth destroying regions (i.e.: in the US, the federal government might take money out of Texas and plow it back into West Virginia). But under the current European political structure, taxing Austria's growth to pay for Italy's bust is simply not an option; which Austrian politicians will want to stand for office on the slogan "let's tax Vienna to send money to Napoli"? (Admittedly, the slogan might work better in Italy).

So what will happen for Italy? Will the ECB cave in and bring in low rates? Will Italy experience a bankruptcy? Or will Italy exit from the Euro?

Divorce, Italian Style was a 1962 movie in which Marcello Mastroianni plays a Sicilian nobleman married to an ugly, bullying and financially ruinous harridan, from whom he desperately wants to disengage. Unfortunately, he has no legal way to do this, since the Italian legal system made no provisions for divorce. His only recourse is therefore to kill his wife.

This movie is, of course, a perfect allegory for the Italian and European economies forty years later. Italy today is under the thumb of an ugly, oppressive and financially ruinous harridan called the Euro. The concept of divorce, separation or withdrawal does not exist under EU law. What, then, is Italy to do?

The fiscal arithmetic which makes Italy's position in a deflationary Euro-zone economically unsustainable is highlighted above. Moreover, politically, the charge that the Euro is responsible for Italy's economic problems is superficially quite easy to sustain (even if it is not actually true). Until 1997, when the socialist government (led by Prodi) took Italy into the Euro, Italy was the fastest growing major economy in Europe, consistently outperforming both Germany and France. Since 1998 it has lagged in every single year behind France and in all but two years behind Germany.

Starting with these economic and political premises one can arrive at a conclusion that the country's continuing membership in the Euro zone will become politically incompatible with the present monetary conditions.

Interestingly, if Italy left the Euro, the government's long-term bonds would continue to pay the present interest of just 3.5%, but now in lira instead of euros. Italy's liabilities would be converted from a strong currency over which it has no control, into a weak currency which it can print at will without any cost to the government or compensating payment to its creditors. This may seem unfair and even fraudulent, but such are the prerogatives of sovereign governments–legal opinion and historical precedent are both quite clear on this point (see below).

To maximize the benefit from this effective debt default, the Italian government would, of course, need to lock in today's Euro interest rates for as long as possible by extending the maturity of its debts before exiting the Euro. This is exactly what the Italian government has been doing. Italy's average debt maturity is now over five years, roughly twice as long as in 1999, and a sensible exit strategy for Italy would be to extend this maturity to ten years or beyond. Luckily for Italy, investors are willing to buy unlimited quantities of long bonds denominated in euros at 3.5% yields.

Now imagine that the Italian government managed to fix all its debts for ten years at 3.5%. It would then face an almost irresistible temptation to ditch the Euro. For suppose that long-term rates on the "New Lira" shot up to 10% immediately after devaluation. The market value of the government's 3.5% debt would instantly be reduced to just 59 cents on the dollar. The market value of Italy's government debt would fall instantly to a manageable 70% of GDP and Italy's fiscal problems would be solved at a stroke.

Looking further ahead, Italians might have to pay higher interest rates on future borrowings. But given that Italy has the world's highest savings rate and very little debt in the private sector, this should not matter too much. The country's fiscal problems are really due to the accumulation of past obligations and breaking out of the Euro could ease this burden overnight.

In sum, the potential benefits of exiting the Euro are quite substantial –and the direct costs may well be smaller than generally believed. But does this mean that a rational government would decide to take the plunge, delaying only for as long as is needed to stretch out the duration of the national debt? Not necessarily, because a third option exists, which is clearly preferable to both the exit strategy and continuation of the status quo. This is to stay in the Euro, but to persuade (or blackmail) the other members and the European Central Bank to pursue aggressive pro-growth policies across the Eurozone as a whole.

Indeed, we are fairly convinced that, come the next economic downturn, one of two things will happen. Either the European Central Bank will have to ease monetary policy decisively to make economic conditions easier for Italy to live with–or Italy will withdraw from the Eurozone. Interestingly, right now, the market is not really pricing in either option. This is thus a very cheap negative carry-trade to put on, with potentially huge returns.

Now the ECB's official statements on monetary policy - that a cut in interest rates or a devaluation would have no effect on economic conditions–are just content-free propaganda: Soviet-style ideology designed to justify whatever happens to be the current policy of the ECB. This is clear not only from common sense but also from the econometric simulations based on past behavior. As the ECB proves slow to ease in a downturn (a fairly safe bet), Italians will be tempted to start rattling their chains and seriously threaten disengagement–which brings us to the question of why an Italian withdrawal should be taken seriously, even though monetary divorce in Europe is not allowed.

To understand this issue we must focus on two unprecedented features of today's monetary arrangements. The first is that the Italian government has, in theory, given up forever a fundamental right of any sovereign country–the right to determine what will constitute legal tender within its own borders. The second is that international investors have assumed this decision to be genuinely irreversible simply because the Maastricht Treaty says it is.

The strange financial result of these two aberrations is that the spread between Italian and German government bond yields is only 55 basis points and that many European banks–unprofitable German mortgage banks in particular–have invested hundreds of billions of Euros on a leveraged basis to pick up the very modest, but apparently risk-free, profits from buying Italian bonds and going short their German equivalents.

As a consequence, a decision by the Italian government to withdraw from the Euro - or even a perception by investors that such a decision might conceivably be threatened by the Italian government sometime in the not too distant future - would trigger a financial crisis of monstrous proportions not only (or even mainly) in Italy, but throughout the Eurozone.

But could Italy credibly threaten to recreate its own currency? So powerful is the dogma that withdrawal is impossible that only two legal scholars have ever seriously examined this issue. They are Professor Hal S. Scott of Harvard Law School (whose 1998 article "*When the Euro Falls Apart*" can be found on the web in the December 1998 issue of *International Finance*) and Dr Charles Proctor of the London lawfirm Nabarro Nathanson, editor of *Mann on the Legal Aspect of Money*, a book described by central bankers as "the Bible" of international monetary law. The latest edition of this book, published by Oxford University Press, contains a new chapter on withdrawal from the Eurozone, which offers the most detailed and thorough analysis of how withdrawal could happen and what it might mean for financial contracts of various kinds.

These two authorities differ substantially in their approach and anyone interested in this subject in detail (which ought to mean anyone with a substantial position in the Euro, European bank shares or European bonds) should read both the articles mentioned above for themselves. Cutting through the detail, there are three points of clear legal consensus which are of huge significance to financial markets:

1. Withdrawal Is Possible

Despite the prohibitions against re-creating national currencies in the EU treaties, the Italian government would have the legal ability to reissue its own currency, even though this would obviously entail financial and economic risks. Sovereign governments can withdraw from treaties, even when some of the provisions purport to be "irrevocable", as in the case of the monetary union. The normal way to do this, is to amend the treaty, but for this to happen all the other signatories (in this case all the other Euro members) would have to agree to allow Italy to withdraw. Such a negotiated withdrawal would sweep away most of the legal obstacles. But what if the other members refused to let Italy leave?

Politically such refusal is hard to imagine. Would other European countries really try to stand in the way of a democratic decision made by the Italian government, especially if this were backed by a referendum? Would Europe's governments deny the Italians a right which Gorbachev granted to the citizens of the former Soviet Union? This seems unlikely.

Nevertheless another option for withdrawal exists. Italy could simply declare unilaterally that it would start printing a New Lira. This action would obviously be in breach of the Maastricht Treaty and would be open to challenge in the European Court of Justice, but it would almost certainly be upheld by Italian courts. The question is what would happen to Italy's domestic and international obligations?

2. Euro Obligations Redenominated into New Lira

In the event of a negotiated withdrawal, there is no doubt that the government would be entitled to rewrite Italian financial contracts, including its own bond obligations, into New Lira. Investors who claimed to be defrauded by such a "redenomination" could expect no support from British or American courts.

The principle of *lex monetae*, a well-established rule of international law which says that monetary contracts should be interpreted by all courts as if they were applying the laws of the issuing country, unless there is specific evidence that the contract was intended to be governed by some foreign law. This means that the judgment of Italian courts as regards domestic securities would be recognised and upheld by other jurisdictions. Because Italian government bonds are issued unequivocally under Italian domestic law, they would be regarded as contracts between Italian residents regardless of who happens to own these bonds today. So courts in London and New York would uphold Italy's right to redenominate government bonds, provided the Italian courts did not strike down the entire currency reform. On the other hand, bonds issued under overseas law - e.g.: Eurobonds under English law or securities under New York law, might not be redenominated and would continue to be paid in Euros.

But what if Italy pulled out of the Euro unilaterally? What if the government created the New Lira by passing a monetary law that was clearly in breach of the (unamended) EU Treaties and therefore illegal under European law? This scenario would create huge uncertainties for investors (and huge opportunities for lawyers). It is impossible to say exactly what would happen.

Detailed discussion of these arguments is probably still premature–and in any case should be left to lawyers–but the financial and policy implications are clear enough: If the possibility of an Italian withdrawal were ever taken seriously by the markets, foreign holders of Italy's € 1.5 trillion public debt would face enormous losses. With nearly 50% of the

Italian public debt held overseas, a good chunk of it by European banks on a leveraged basis with a zero capital-weighting, the potential losses from an Italian redenomination would be big enough to endanger the solvency of the entire Eurozone banking system. **In other words, the Italian government is now in a position to kill the Euro and wreck the European banking system merely by *threatening* to withdraw.**

The most likely result of such a threat would be to force the ECB to ease policy and encourage a weaker Euro, in order to accommodate the Italian government's demands. This would certainly be a rational response from the ECB.

But what if the ECB failed to play ball? Or what if Italy's economic conditions, following the coming tax hikes, deteriorate further? The government could then become desperate enough to start openly demanding a monetary easing and devaluation, as it did in 1992. That time round, the Bundesbank decided to ignore the Italian (and British) entreaties and orchestrated the expulsion of the lira and the pound from the ERM. This time, however, the balance of power is tilted the other way. The Italian government can blackmail the ECB with the threat of withdrawal and a European banking crisis.

The ECB's top priorities would then be to prevent a collapse of the entire Euro project or a solvency crisis among the German/European banks. Given this shift in the balance of power it seems almost inevitable that the Italians would win the confrontation and that the ECB would have to ease.

Of course, at present, such speculations are still just fantasy, or at least economic science fiction. But anybody who still believes that a break-up of the Euro is impossible should at least re-examine this assumption with a skeptical eye. And investors would do well to remember that **experience shows that, in confrontations between politics and financial markets, events sometimes move from impossible to inevitable without ever passing through improbable.**

In any event, Italy's precarious position within a shoddily-built, politically motivated, Euro monetary experiments certainly raises doubt about the "sustainability" of the current global financial arrangements. And unfortunately, Italy is not the only dark horse in Europe. Investors who want to be better prepared for the "impossible" than they were before the 1992 European currency crisis should contact Oxford University Press for a copy of _Mann and the Legal Aspect of Money_ (and those who would rather eschew a 900-page legal textbook, should at least rent a video of _Divorce Italian Style_).

Investment Conclusions

Most of us naturally suffer from vertigo. So with most equity markets around the world (except Japan) still not so far from all-time highs, it is only normal to want to look down and fear a potential rapid decline. This is all the more true since, of late, the news flow has hardly been that positive.

Of course, as with other instinctual tendencies of human beings, a whole industry has sprung up to feed this fear. Indeed, while equity markets never go up in a straight line, over time, they do tend to rise. Yet, when we read industry economists and strategists, we find that 90% of the work out there (we picked this number out of thin air, but it felt right to us) is devoted to trying to guess when the next market meltdown will occur, and only 10% of the work (at most) is done to explain why we should expect equity markets to move higher, why the world keeps getting better, why capitalism works, etc... This is an odd quandary: why would so many bright people decide to "challenge" the long-term market's trend and the history of capitalism to forecast doom and gloom?

We recently asked this question over dinner to our good friend Victor Niederhoffer (the author of the must-read book, *Practical Speculation*), and we found his answer compelling: *Ayn Rand used to talk of 'second-handers': those who derive their self-esteem from the perceptions of others, not from objective achievements. One virulent form of second-handedness masquerades as virtue: the need to be needed. I suspect it's behind the overly-chivalrous and boastful demeanor of some elderly gentlemen. It is also behind the pessimism.*

The doomsayer needs followers who feel endangered and vulnerable. The forecasts of doom make the prophet needed to get through the pending calamity. No one needs a savior if the forecast is for sunny times ahead. By undercutting the sense of security of others, the doomsayer carves out a niche for himself: I will get you through the market panic, the economic collapse, etc. The confident, optimistic investor is the doomsayer's greatest threat. To become needed, they must make others needy. Such is their benevolence.

Twenty years after 1987, we stand at new highs on global equities, and the doomsayers continue to beat their drum. It is odd how we excoriate those who encouraged people to buy stock in 2000, but yet say nothing about those who counseled against equity ownership for the last 10,000 Dow points.

If a physician sickened his patients in order to have a steady stream of revenues, no one would hesitate to call it malpractice. But what of investment advisors who fill their clients with fear in order to sell them services and seminars?

'You need not examine a folly', Rand once wrote; 'you merely need to identify what it accomplishes'. Pessimism and negativity create dependency and a psychological crippling. The need to be needed is a need to undercut the certainty and security of others. That's why it's a 'symptom of something worse'."

Which brings us back to the question at hand: should we be pessimistic today? Undeniably, there are serious reasons to be concerned:

-   The financial revolution has hit a serious road-bump and will likely detract more from growth than contribute to economic activity for the foreseeable future.

-   The credit crunch which has crippled the US economy in the past six months is only now starting to unfold in Europe and its effect there could be far more devastating than investors anticipate (on that note, is it not interesting that the majority of financial institutions that have lined up to recapitalize Ambac, the troubled monoline insurer, are European? Does this not tell us that they would be the most damaged by an Ambac bankruptcy?).

- We continue to see, through rising oil prices, an ever greater amount of wealth transferred from market players to non-market players (i.e.: oil money to Venezuela, Iran or Saudi Arabia; growth in Russian reserves etc…). This is rarely conducive to faster growth.

- Until Asian and Middle Eastern central banks decide to bite the bullet and stop manipulating their currencies, inflation in our part of the world may very well continue to accelerate, prompting counter-productive price-control measures, constraints on bank lending etc…

Still, for every reason to be negative, there are reasons to be positive. These reasons include the fact that more people are getting richer, and freer, than the world has ever seen, and all at the same time. The fact that these people all around the world are communicating, and exchanging ideas and goods in a way that would have been deemed impossible just a few years ago. The fact that companies are having to run ever faster, and become ever more efficient to survive and thrive. For most managements, complacency is no longer the option it was twenty years ago.

For all these reasons, I maintain a fairly "bulled-up" portfolio. For my own money, I happen to be:

a) Long Asian real estate and Asian currencies. This gives me exposure to the second structural mega-trend described in this book.

b) Long companies exposed to the growth of Asian consumption. On this front, most, though not all, of the companies I own are based in Asia.

c) Long companies exposed to the continuation of the global infrastructure spending boom.

d) Very long a portfolio of global "platform companies" whose R&D spending ensures that they will be amongst tomorrow leaders, as identified by our research. These companies tend to be focused in the technology, health care, consumer cyclical, consumer staples and financial services. As things stand, and for valuation reasons, a lot of these companies happen to be in the US. I like the fact that, in the US, I can buy today cheap equities in an undervalued currency. More importantly, this basket of stocks gives me exposure to the third and fourth mega-trends described above.

e) Long Japanese REITS, denominated in Yen and SG$ (thus far, this has not been the best-performing part of my portfolio.)

f) Long protection on European banks and European sovereigns. In my view, if an accident is going to take place, it will be here. Investors over the past decade have just grown too complacent about Europe's internal contradictions.

This portfolio did well enough in 2006 and 2007. Needless to say, in 2008, it is off to a rough start, apart, interestingly, from the last position. In the first quarter, the blow-out in European spreads helped salvage what would otherwise have been a tough quarter for the personal P&L...

So yes, I remain optimistic and look to the future with enthusiasm. All the while remembering what my friend Clay Allen never tires of telling me: "Remember Louis, money managers are not paid to forecast. Money managers are paid to adapt." Unfortunately, adapting to this ever-rapidly changing world of ours is not always easy. Yet, there is no other recipe to making money in today's financial markets.

ISBN: 978-988-99752-3-4